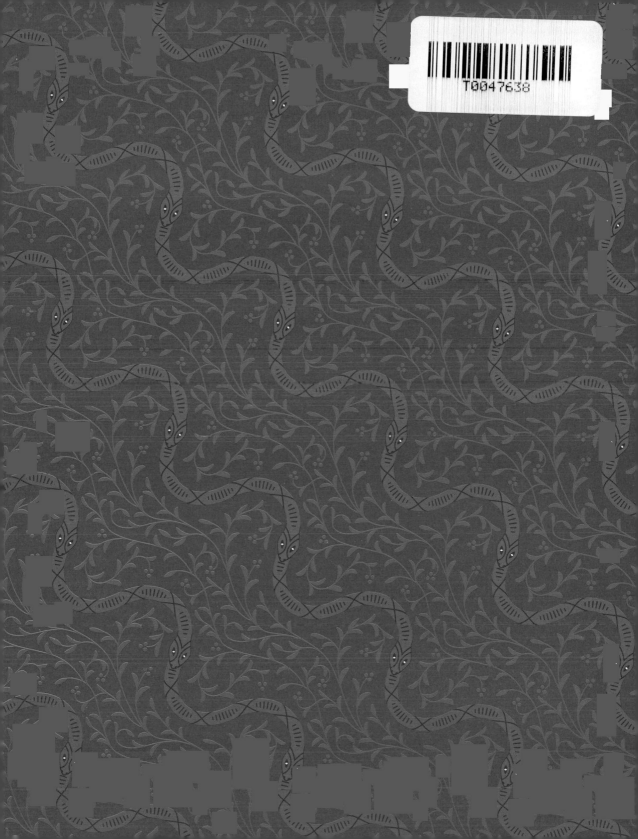

THE CONSPIRACY BOOK

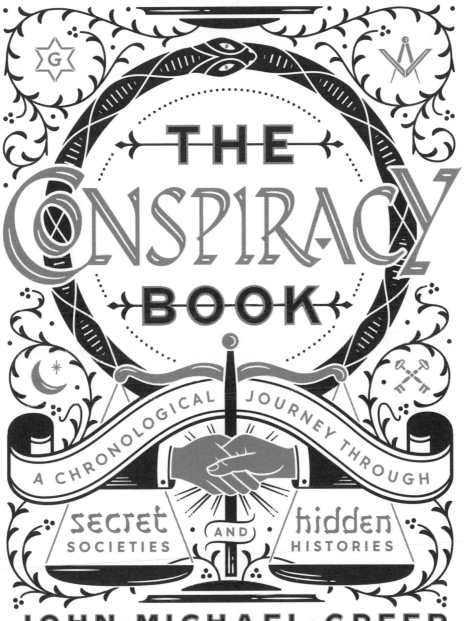

THE CONSPIRACY BOOK

A CHRONOLOGICAL JOURNEY THROUGH

secret SOCIETIES AND hidden HISTORIES

JOHN·MICHAEL·GREER

UNION SQUARE & CO.

NEW YORK

**UNION
SQUARE
& CO.**

NEW YORK

UNION SQUARE & CO. and the distinctive Union Square & Co. logo are
trademarks of Sterling Publishing Co., Inc.

Union Square & Co., LLC, is a subsidiary of Sterling Publishing Co., Inc.

ISBN 978-1-4549-3004-4

For information about custom editions, special sales, and premium purchases,
please contact specialsales@unionsquareandco.com.

Printed in Malaysia

6 8 10 9 7 5

unionsquareandco.com

Cover design and illustration by Spencer Charles
Endpaper illustration by Frances MacLeod
For image credits, see page 211

"This is the real history of secret societies in the Western world—a fascinating tapestry of forgotten struggles and lost causes, of hidden groups of men and women who pursued agendas that would one day triumph, and of others laboring just as hard for agendas that would end only in oblivion."

—John Michael Greer, from the Introduction

CONTENTS

ONSPIRACY IS AS OLD AS THE HUMAN race. A million years ago, when our distant ancestors were still adapting to the vast climate changes that forced them down out of the trees, ambitious young prehumans doubtless made plans to go out hunting with a dominant elder and put a spear through his back. The plot hatched in secret, the arrangements made out of sight of watchful eyes, the sudden act that no one but the plotters expects: these are in our bones and our blood, part of what it means to be human.

The organized secret society, though, is a far more recent thing. The Roman senators who plotted the assassination of Julius Caesar in 43 BCE, for example, didn't found a society that met in secret for years afterward; they planned Caesar's death, carried out the plan, and then tried and failed to seize power openly. A long series of events, beginning in the Middle Ages, was needed to lay the foundations for the rise of secret societies as a significant historical reality. Then, when the conditions were right, it took an improbable collision between two very different things—a men's social club with an exotic origin, and an exiled royal house scrambling for a way back into power—to kick-start the golden age of secret societies.

The men's social club was Freemasonry: the Ancient and Honorable Society of Free and Accepted Masons, to give it its full title.

Freemasonry started off in the Middle Ages as a craft guild in the building trades, not much different from the guilds of butchers, bakers, candlestick makers, and other trades that managed economic life in medieval Europe. Guilds had initiation rituals, regular meetings, and oaths of membership that bound initiates not to reveal certain trade secrets to outsiders—all features that would be useful in the secret societies of the future.

Economic changes at the end of the Middle Ages swept most guilds into oblivion. The stonemasons' guild survived in Britain by turning itself into a social club, inviting men who were not stonemasons to join as "Accepted Masons." (We would call them "honorary members" today.) By 1700, most members in most of the stonemasons' lodges in Britain were Accepted Masons rather than builders, and the lodges had begun to attract wealthy and influential members, who found Freemasonry a useful source of social connections.

That was when the other ingredient in the rise of secret societies entered the mix: the House of Stuart, the former royal house of Britain, thrown out of power in a revolution in 1688 and replaced by the House of Hanover. Supporters of the House of Stuart were called Jacobites after Jacobus, the Latin version of the name of the deposed King James II. All through the first half of the eighteenth century, they carried on a campaign of subversion and propaganda against the new Hanoverian government, and twice—in 1715 and 1745—launched rebellions in the name of the Stuart cause. After the defeat of the 1715 rising, the Jacobites set out to use every available means to undermine the House of Hanover, and in the process they infiltrated Freemasonry and launched several new branches of it as a cover for their activities.

The Jacobites failed, and Freemasonry soon returned to its enduring role as a charitable and social society for men, but the idea of using secret societies to overthrow unpopular governments caught on. Over the course of the eighteenth century, secret societies

Lithograph of Freemason emblems and symbols, c. 1872.

sprang up all over Europe. The outbreak of the French Revolution in 1789 threw this process into overdrive, and for the next century—the golden age of secret societies—conspiracies from every point on the political spectrum pushed their own agendas using the classic toolkit of the secret society.

In the United States, secret societies found a home early on. The Revolutionary War was launched by two secret societies—the Committees of Correspondence and the Sons of Liberty—and plenty of other conspiracies and secret organizations tried to promote their causes and undercut their opponents from that point on. It was quite literally true for many years that for every secret society, there was an equal and opposite secret society.

The fear of secret societies rose in parallel with secret societies themselves. Not all the fears that were splashed over eighteenth- and nineteenth-century mass media were based on realities, though. Demagogues at various points on the political spectrum discovered the uses of whipping their listeners into a panic over the supposed activities of secret societies. Outright frauds and fabrications also won their share of public attention.

One ironic result of the rise of anti–secret-society agitation was a vast exaggeration of the power, effectiveness, and age of secret societies themselves. From the beginning, secret societies had been claiming to be bigger, older, and stronger than they actually were, since this helped them attract members. The opponents of secret societies found similarly that it was easier to attract members to their crusade if they exaggerated the size, age, and power of the secret societies they were fighting. By the late twentieth century, as a result, bestselling books and widely watched documentaries splashed around wild claims about secret societies and conspiracies, and succeeded mostly in obscuring the fascinating reality behind the claims.

“ The plot hatched in secret, the arrangements made out of sight of watchful eyes, the sudden act that no one but the plotters expects: these are in our bones and our blood, part of what it means to be human. ”

What has been missed in all the hullaballoo is that *secrecy is a tool of the weak.* People turn to conspiracy when they don't have the political, economic, or cultural influence to pursue their goals by more direct means. When a secret society gathers enough power to push its agenda in public, it promptly morphs into a political party, an army, or a government. That was what happened to the Committees of Correspondence and the Sons of Liberty after 1775, when the cause of American independence had won enough support in the thirteen colonies to make the Revolution possible. Scores of other secret societies down through the years made the same transition once they were strong enough, but there were always many more that never managed to accomplish their goals, and faded out of existence as times changed.

For nearly three centuries, therefore, secret societies provided a setting where new movements for radical change found a home and began the long struggle to make their dreams a reality. Some of the dreams of secret societies turned out to be nightmares: both the Nazi Party and the Communist movement, for example, started out as secret societies, succeeded in making the transition to real power, and splashed the twentieth century with the blood of millions. Other secret societies pursued more humane goals, seeking to liberate their homelands from foreign overlords, to push democratic reforms onto oppressive regimes, or in some cases to oppose secret societies with toxic goals by turning their own methods against them.

This is the real history of secret societies in the Western world—a fascinating tapestry of forgotten struggles and lost causes, of hidden groups of men and women who pursued agendas that would one day triumph, and of others laboring just as hard for agendas that would end only in oblivion. It is a history that has contributed more than most people realize to the world we live in today. *The Conspiracy Book* is the password and secret sign that will open that history to you.

עזרת הגוים מחוץ לחיל
VOORHOF DER HEYDENEN.
Gedrukt by J: Danckerts met Privilegie

THE TEMPLE OF SOLOMON

I N THE TENTH CENTURY BCE, THE MIDDLE East was a patchwork of little kingdoms, hundreds of them, each with its own language, culture, and religion, each centered on a national temple where priests offered sacrifices to the local god or goddess. The kingdom of Israel was just one more of these tiny nations, and when King Solomon of Israel (c. 970–931 BCE) built a temple in Jerusalem for his people's guardian deity, it was such a standard project that he was able to ask his ally King Hiram of Tyre (c. 1000–c. 946 BCE) to send trained builders and metalworkers for the job. Nor was the temple he built on a hill just north of the original city of Jerusalem anything out of the ordinary: a plain rectangular building with stone walls and a wooden roof, ninety feet long, thirty feet wide, and forty-five feet high, covered with a thin layer of hammered gold.

Two thousand years later, the collected legends of Solomon's little kingdom had become the Old Testament of a major world religion. In medieval Europe, as economic activity sprang back to life after the long crisis of the Dark Ages, local guilds of tradesmen borrowed stories from the Bible and the lives of the saints as raw material for the simple ceremonies by which new members were initiated. A guild of stonemasons somewhere in the British Isles, probably but not certainly in what is now Scotland, adopted the story of the building of King Solomon's temple for that purpose. Other stonemasons' guilds had different rituals, focusing on such other stories as the building of the Tower of Babel. Many centuries later, however, as stonemasons' guilds in Britain began to mutate into something very different, the ritual about the building of the Temple of Solomon would become the core initiation ceremony of Freemasonry.

SEE ALSO: The Regius Manuscript (c. 1390), Rituals of Brothering (1639)

The bustling courtyard of the temple of Solomon, in a seventeenth-century etching by Johan Danckerts.

PYTHAGORAS.

ΠΥΘΑΓΟΡΗΣ ΣΑΜΙΩΝ

Apud Fuluium Vrsinum
in nomismate æreo.

THE PYTHAGOREAN BROTHERHOOD

IN THE SIXTH CENTURY BCE, THE CITY OF Crotona in southern Italy was a booming Greek colony, a center of new economic and intellectual ventures. That's where Pythagoras (c. 570–c. 495 BCE) settled when he finished his travels across the ancient world in search of wisdom. The inventor of the word *philosopher* and a brilliant mathematician, Pythagoras was also a mystic, and the organization he founded—the Pythagorean Brotherhood—taught a complex system of thought in which geometry, vegetarianism, and reincarnation played important roles.

While it drew some of its features from older Greek social institutions and others from the temples of Egypt where Pythagoras had studied, the Pythagorean Brotherhood was something new in the Western world. Its members joined voluntarily, took oaths of secrecy and obedience to the organization, and rose gradually up through the order's ranks, learning its teachings and secrets step by step as they proceeded. That same pattern would become the standard template for secret societies in centuries to come.

The brotherhood drew much of its membership from Crotona's wealthy upper class, and so it inevitably got entangled in the bitter struggles between aristocratic and populist parties that shook the Greek world during the sixth century BCE. Around 500 BCE, those struggles spawned savage riots in Crotona and several nearby cities. During the riots, many members of the brotherhood barricaded themselves inside its Crotona headquarters and died when the rioters burned the building to the ground. Pythagoras himself escaped to the nearby town of Metapontum, where he died a few years later. Other survivors scattered across the Greek world, bearing Pythagorean teachings and the idea of a secret, oath-bound organization with them.

SEE ALSO: The Gnostics (1st century CE)

A line engraving of Pythagoras. Pythagoras is credited with inventing the word *philosophy*. As a mathematician—perhaps the greatest in history—he is most widely known as the author of the Pythagorean theorem. His teachings had a profound influence on philosophers Socrates, Plato, and Aristotle.

THE GNOSTICS

THEY CALLED THEMSELVES "THE PEOPLE OF knowledge"—that is what *Gnostikoi* means in ancient Greek—and all through the first few centuries of the Christian era, they could be found all over the Roman Empire and beyond it. No one is sure exactly when or where the first Gnostic teachings emerged, or who founded their faith. The Gnostics themselves taught that their faith was the true teaching of Jesus Christ, which had been suppressed by the established churches but flourished in secret.

To the Gnostics, salvation was a matter not of faith but of personal knowledge. The universe, they believed, was the creation of an evil power, the Demiurge, and human souls were imprisoned there, far from their true home in the eternal world of light. Jesus had come from the world of light to teach the secret knowledge that would set souls free— the knowledge of their true nature as beings of the world of light, and the rituals, medi-

tations, and practices that would free them from the world of matter once and for all.

Gnosticism originally emerged in the tolerant religious climate of the Roman world, and it flourished through the first three centuries of the Christian era. Once the mainstream Christian church seized political power in the Roman world, however, Gnosticism was declared heretical, and Gnostics risked being imprisoned, exiled, or executed for their beliefs.

The obvious solution was to go underground. For more than a thousand years thereafter, Gnostic sects concealed themselves from Church authorities and passed on their teachings only in secret, to recruits who had been carefully vetted for discretion and loyalty. In the process, they laid a foundation on which future secret societies would build.

SEE ALSO: The Cathars (1030)

Early Christian Gnostics denoted Abraxas, an enigmatic and mystical creature, as the Demiurge and creator of the universe. The Abraxas often was shown with a rooster's head to represent vigilance. The whip and shield symbolize power and protective wisdom, respectively. In the thirteenth century, it was common for the Knights Templar to use seals bearing the image of Abraxas.

et frere au ieune gautier qui estoit homs ac
ses dignes de louenge et asses nobles et renom
mes ou palais du roy.

De la croiserie talbigois et de la noble vic
toire simou le conte de mont fort vuj.

THE CATHARS

ALL THROUGH THE MIDDLE AGES, RELIgion dominated life in the Western world to an extent that is hard to imagine today, and so the secret groups that emerged in those years were almost all religious in nature. One of the most important was the Cathar movement, which emerged in Italy in the eleventh century. The first known Cathar congregation was in Monteforte, Italy, and existed by 1030.

The name *Cathar* comes from the Greek word for "pure." Their enemies called them the Albigensians, "those people from Albi," after a city in France where they had an early presence. Their faith, however, came straight out of ancient Gnosticism. They believed that human souls came from a world of light but had been trapped in the material world by the trickery of the Devil, and that Christ had come to show the imprisoned souls the way to escape. Like most Gnostic sects, they admitted women to the clergy and had a more relaxed attitude toward sex than their Catholic adversaries—Cathar clergy vowed themselves to poverty, celibacy, and vegetarianism, but ordinary believers were free of such restrictions.

The Cathar movement was secret in its early days, but by 1200 it had become the majority faith in southern France and abandoned the cloak of secrecy. This proved to be a disastrous mistake. In 1209 the pope proclaimed a crusade against the Cathars. Over the next thirty-five years, the South of France was ravaged by Catholic armies in a bloodbath that reduced the population of the region by more than half, and the Cathar movement was effectively destroyed. The brutality of the response convinced many other alternative religious movements that total secrecy was necessary to their survival.

SEE ALSO: The Gnostics (1st century CE), The Adamites (1400)

This illustration from *Les Grandes chroniques de France* (The major chronicles of France), c. 1350, depicts the expulsion of Cathars from Carcassone, France, in 1209, during the Albigensian Crusade. The bloodbath lasted for about thirty-five years and effectively destroyed the Cathar movement.

Exécution de Jacques Molay, grand-maître des Templiers.

FALL OF THE KNIGHTS TEMPLAR

THE ORDER OF KNIGHTS TEMPLAR, A GREAT European order of knighthood, was not a secret society. Founded in 1118 by nine crusading knights, it became rich and influential. By the fourteenth century, its wealth had made it a tempting prize for greedy monarchs, and the defeat of the Christian side in the Crusades deprived the Knights Templar of its official reason for existence. While the Grand Master of the order, Jacques de Molay (c. 1243–1314), lobbied the kings of Europe for a new Crusade, one of those kings—Philip IV of France (1268–1314)—made plans of his own.

On Friday, October 13, 1307, royal officials across France raided Templar properties in the kingdom and arrested every Templar they could find. The charge was heresy. The captive Templars were tortured to make them confess to a laundry list of crimes. The following year, Pope Clement V (c. 1264–1314) ordered Templars throughout Europe arrested, and in 1312 the Knights Templar order was dissolved by the Council of Vienne.

Most of the order's members were allowed to join other monastic orders, but Jacques de Molay and sixty other knights were burned at the stake. According to legend, de Molay called on Philip and Clement to join him before God's tribunal. If so, the curse was effective, for king and pope were both dead within a year.

Legend also had it that some Templars escaped arrest and sought refuge in Scotland, and that Freemasonry descends in part from the heritage of the Templars. Whether this was true or not, it helped shape a future age of conspiracies against political and religious absolutism.

SEE ALSO: Ramsay's Oration (1736), The Strict Observance (1754), The Convention of Wilhelmsbad (1782), The French Revolution (1789)

In this eighteenth-century wood engraving by Jacques-Louis David, the last Grand Master of the Knights Templars, Jacques de Molay, is pictured being burned alive at the stake in Paris in 1314, having been charged with heresy.

THE REGIUS MANUSCRIPT

THESE WORDS COME FROM THE OLDEST surviving set of rules for master stonemasons in Britain. They were copied by hand around 1390 and bound into a book, which became part of the library of the kings of England around the beginning of the sixteenth century, and now forms part of the collection of the British Library. Historians call it the Regius Manuscript.

In 1390, the stonemasons' guilds in Britain were ordinary trade organizations of a kind found all over medieval Europe. Like guilds in other trades, they regulated hours, working conditions, and the training of workmen, and also provided charitable services to their members and the community. They had a great deal of traditional symbolism and ornate initiation rituals for new apprentices, workmen, and masters, but this was also true of other guilds—even those with no claim to a connection with the Knights Templar.

In the centuries that followed the penning of the Regius Manuscript, however, the guild system fell apart, swept aside by new conditions as Britain embraced a market economy. Most guilds went out of existence. The stonemasons' guilds managed to survive by bringing in new members from outside the building trades. In the process, they morphed into Freemasonry and established the template on which nearly all later secret societies would be built.

SEE ALSO: The Schaw Statutes (1598), The First Masonic Grand Lodge (1717)

The Regius Manuscript is the oldest known record of the craft of masonry, dating from 1390. Written in verse, as an epic poem, the manuscript was probably composed by a priest or monk who was familiar with older Masonic documents.

ASSEMBLÉES nocturnes des ADAMITES.

F. Morellon la Cave Sculp.

THE ADAMITES

THE CATHARS WERE FAR FROM THE ONLY medieval religious secret society to help set the stage for the great age of conspiracies to come. Another example was the Adamite movement, which was founded in what is now the Czech Republic around 1400 by a visionary named Picard. Convinced that he had been chosen by God to lead humanity back to Paradise, Picard renamed himself Adam, Son of God, and announced that since Christ came to free humanity from sin, all true believers were incapable of sinning.

His followers accordingly considered all members to be priests, worshiped in the nude, and practiced sexual promiscuity, insisting "to the pure, all things are pure." Such customs offered female converts opportunities for leadership roles and sexual satisfaction that were rarely available to women in medieval society, and the Adamite movement accordingly became a significant presence all through central and western Europe in the late Middle Ages.

The Catholic Church responded to the movement in its usual heavy-handed way, and many hundreds of Adamites were tried and burned at the stake for heresy in the fifteenth and sixteenth centuries. The movement regrouped by going underground, becoming a secret society with signs of recognition, secret meetings in the homes of members, and recruitment through personal contacts. These arrangements proved successful enough that the Adamite movement under various names survived for at least three centuries. Later secret societies would borrow many of the same features for their own uses.

SEE ALSO: The Alumbrados (1511)

The Adamite movement was based on the idea that all true believers in Christ are incapable of sinning. Consequently, all followers, both men and women, were considered to be priests. The movement had a liberating effect on its constituents, who worshipped in the nude, as seen in this etching by François Morellon la Cave (1696–1768).

THE ALUMBRADOS

MARIA DE SANTO DOMINGO (C. 1480–1524) was the most harmless of religious visionaries. A devout Spanish Catholic from the little town of Piedrahita near Toledo, she became convinced that the human soul could achieve holiness by emptying itself of thoughts and desires and focusing its attention entirely on God. She began to teach her ideas in Toledo in 1511, and quickly won a following among local Catholics. Those who accepted her teachings called themselves the Alumbrados—Spanish for "the illuminated ones."

Over on the other side of the planet, a very similar set of ideas played a central role in Zen Buddhism, but that tradition emerged in a far more tolerant religious environment than that which Maria de Santo Domingo faced. Her venture into Catholic Zen promptly landed her in trouble with church officials, who took exception to her teachings on various points of doctrine and called in the Inquisition. While she herself managed to avoid the stake, many of her followers were tortured and burned as heretics in the years that followed.

The gentle rise and brutal fall of the Alumbrados would have been just another footnote in the long history of religious intolerance in the Western world, except for one small detail—the name that Maria's followers chose for themselves. Translated into Latin, the phrase "illuminated ones" is *illuminati*. Centuries later, after the French Revolution, conspiracy theorists trying to pin the blame for the turmoil of those years on a very different secret society—the Bavarian Illuminati—used the coincidence of names to claim that the Bavarian order had existed since the Middle Ages.

SEE ALSO: The Illuminés of Avignon (1770), The Bavarian Illuminati (1776)

A contemporary photo of the city skyline of Toledo, Spain, where the founder of the Alumbrados, Maria de Santo Domingo, began teaching her ideas.

יהוה   EMMANVEL.

Liefte ·   Waerheit ·

Vnſe Herte, is Godes Gemöt.
Vnſe Weſen lieflick, alſe de Lelie ſöt.
Vnſe Trûwe / Liefte / vnde Waerheit,
Is Godes Licht / Leuen / vnde Klaerheit.

E. M.

THE FAMILY OF LOVE

ANOTHER INFLUENTIAL RELIGIOUS secret society, the Family of Love was founded in 1555 by the German mystic Heinrich Nicolai. Its members believed that experiencing the love of God was more important than believing in an officially approved set of doctrines, and held that the Bible ought to be interpreted as an allegory of the soul's relationship with God rather than taken literally. In the hothouse religious atmosphere of the sixteenth century, that was enough to get the Family denounced, condemned, and imprisoned or exiled. As a result, the Familists (as Nicolai's followers were called) went underground.

Familists thus concealed their membership and attended the officially approved church services of countries in which they lived. They recruited new members quietly, sounding out potential converts in advance, and not mentioning the phrase "Family of Love" until the new recruit had proven his or her readiness to keep the secret. By these methods, the Family spread throughout England, the Netherlands, and northern Germany, despite the efforts of more orthodox religious bodies to keep them in check.

With the coming of the seventeenth century, as Europe dissolved into savage religious warfare, the Familist movement faded out, though its ideas became widespread all through the radical religious scene of the time. The Family may also have played a role in inspiring the Rosicrucian movement. Certainly its use of secrecy and concealment were copied by many other organizations, as religious struggles gave way to political and economic conflicts in the centuries immediately ahead.

SEE ALSO: The Rosicrucians (1614)

A print made by Hans Ladenspelder, c. 1574, thought to have been used to illustrate the "Family of Love" books.

THE SCHAW STATUTES

WILLIAM SCHAW (C. 1550–1602), THE younger son of a Scottish laird, grew up at the Scottish royal court and became one of King James VI's trusted servants. In 1583, the king appointed him to the office of Master of Works, with authority over all royal building projects in Scotland. Carrying out the duties of that office brought Schaw into contact with lodges of stonemasons all over the Scottish kingdom.

By 1583, however, the old stonemasons' guilds were in disarray, hammered by sweeping economic changes and the violent religious controversies that swept Europe at that time. Schaw therefore decided to issue a set of regulations to be followed by master stonemasons throughout Scotland. The regulations, later called the Schaw Statutes, appeared in 1598; a longer version with some changes was issued the following year.

The Schaw Statutes had only a modest impact on the stonemasons' guilds, even in Scotland, because by the time they were issued, the entire guild system was coming apart at the seams as the end of the Middle Ages brought sweeping economic changes to Europe. Within a century, stonemasons, like skilled artisans in other trades, would be independent businessmen who no longer worked under the authority of a guild. Most guilds simply dissolved, but a few survived by transforming themselves and taking on new roles.

The stonemasons' guilds, as has been alluded to earlier, chose this latter path and began the process that turned them into modern Freemasonry, a men's social club and charitable society, and the template on which most secret societies were based. As a marker of these changes, the Schaw Statutes are crucial, because they offer a glimpse at Freemasonry on the eve of its great transformation.

SEE ALSO: The Regius Manuscript (c. 1390), Elias Ashmole Becomes a Mason (1646)

Freemasonry drew its symbols from stonemason's tools, among them the compass and square ruler. Note the "all-seeing eye of god," a symbol of antiquity, meant to represent divine watchfulness over all our deeds and actions.

THE ROSICRUCIANS

THE PRINTING PRESS WAS THE INTERNET of early modern Europe, and the torrent of books, pamphlets, and broadsheets that poured from print shops all over Europe had at least as dramatic an impact on the culture of the time as websites and online forums have today. Thus, it's not surprising that one of the most enduring themes in the entire history of conspiracies came out of a pamphlet published by a small German press in 1614. Its title was *Fama Fraternitatis*, Latin for "News of the Fraternity," and it announced the existence of a secret society called the Fraternity of the Rose Cross.

According to the *Fama*, the Fraternity had been founded in the fifteenth century by a mysterious sage named C.R.C., and knew all the secrets of mysticism, alchemy, and healing. Its members moved silently through society, pledged to heal the sick free of charge, and met at a secret college somewhere in Germany, where the tomb of C.R.C. was located.

The *Fama* inspired many attempts to find the Fraternity and also attracted denunciations from religious authorities. Two more publications, the *Confession of the Fraternity* and *The Chemical Wedding of Christian Rosenkreutz*, roused more interest. For a while, the Rosicrucians, as members of the fellowship came to be called, were a hot topic in European popular culture.

It's ironic that all the evidence suggests that the *Fama* was an elaborate practical joke cooked up by a circle of college students at the University of Tübingen, who had no idea they were about to launch one of the great themes in the history of secret societies. No doubt they would have been stunned to learn that several competing organizations, all claiming to be the genuine original Rosicrucians, are still active today.

SEE ALSO: The Golden and Rosy Cross (1755)

A satirical rendering of the Collegium Fraternitatis, by Theophilus Schweighardt Constantiens, 1618. Newly converted Rosicrucians might be dismayed (or amused) to learn that a group of college kids from Tübingen, Germany, in 1614, may have cooked up the *Fama Fraternitatis*— the Rosicrucian manifesto—as a practical joke!

Plate 9

delin.

Eng.ᵈ & Pubᵈ May 7, 1799 by J. Baldrey, Cambridge

Swift's advice to Servants,

"While your Master is saying grace, take the chairs from behind the Company, and go out."

RITUALS OF BROTHERING

NOWHERE IN EUROPE DID THE RELIGIOUS struggles of the sixteenth and seventeenth centuries have a more drastic social impact than in Scotland, where the colorful Catholicism of the Middle Ages was swept away by the puritanical Calvinist faith. Many traditional Scots customs were prohibited in the years that followed, and one of those was the old custom of brothering.

Traditionally, new servants hired into a household and new apprentices taken on by a master went through a brothering ceremony to welcome them into their new place. Customs varied by place and profession, but generally involved pranks and horseplay, generally ending with the newcomer being made to "shake the Devil's hand"—the hand in question being an object covered in thick hair—and having his head "washed" by having water and whiskey poured over it. The ceremony ended with a round of drinks for all, paid for by the newcomer.

All this was anathema to the dour Calvinists who ruled Scotland in the seventeenth century, and so laws were promptly passed outlawing the custom. In 1639, in one of the first records of brothering, the Scottish Privy Council issued an edict prohibiting brothering among servants on account of the "drinking, ryot, and excesse" involved. Similar regulations were issued repeatedly during the seventeenth and eighteenth centuries, with little effect.

The rituals of brothering, raucous and informal as they were, ended up having a major impact once the golden age of secret societies began. Among the crafts that practiced such rituals of initiation were the stonemasons—and in the years following the Privy Council's edict, that guild would begin its fateful transformation into Freemasonry.

SEE ALSO: The Regius Manuscript (c. 1390), The Schaw Statues (1598)

The stonemasons would eventually absorb initiation rituals inspired by traditional Scots customs, such as brothering, which involved pranks like the one pictured here. In this humorous illustration from *Directions to Servants*, a satirical essay by Jonathan Swift (1667–1745) published after his death, servants are literally pulling the chairs out from under their master and his guests.

ELIAS ASHMOLE BECOMES
A FREEMASON

THE END OF THE ENGLISH CIVIL WAR IN 1646 left Elias Ashmole (1617–1692) at loose ends. A scholar and astrologer, he had joined the Royalist side when Parliamentary armies threatened Oxford, and served with distinction in the army during the war's endgame, as the Royalist cause collapsed and King Charles I (1600–1649) became a prisoner of Parliament. Once the fighting ended and the Royalist army was disbanded, Ashmole went to stay with relatives in Cheshire and tried to figure out what to do with his life.

In the autumn of that year, though, an unexpected opportunity appeared. An ancient guild of stonemasons, he learned, had begun to open its doors to "accepted members"—men of good character who were not employed in the building trades, but were interested in symbolism and ritual and willing to accept the social and charitable obligations of brothers of the guild. Ashmole eagerly applied for admission, and on October 12, 1646, he and his brother-in-law Henry Mainwaring (1587–1653) became the first two accepted Freemasons in England.

That initiation turned out to have immense importance for the history of Masonry. In 1660, Charles's son returned from exile to become England's king. The new King Charles II (1630–1685) rewarded Ashmole's loyalty to the Royalist cause by supporting him financially and helping to promote his scholarly works. Ashmole had remained an active Freemason ever since that October evening, and his rise to prominence and royal favor brought extensive publicity to the Craft. In the decades after 1660, as a result, Freemasonry completed its transformation from a medieval stoneworkers' guild to an initiatory organization that attracted men of many different classes and backgrounds.

SEE ALSO: The Schaw Statutes (1598), The First Masonic Grand Lodge (1717)

A late seventeenth-century painting of Elias Ashmole by John Riley. Ashmole was one of the first to apply and be admitted to the Freemasons in England. His initiation was significant on a number of levels. Perhaps the most important was that it signaled the transition of Freemasonry from a medieval stonemasons' guild to an organization that drew its constituents from diverse social classes.

THE GLORIOUS REVOLUTION

JAMES II (1633–1701), THE BROTHER AND successor of King Charles II (1630–1685) of Great Britain, was neither a bad man nor a particularly bad king. He had, however, two catastrophic strikes against him. The first was that he had converted to Catholicism while he and his family were in exile in France after the English Civil War; the second was that he wanted to follow the lead of France's King Louis XIV (1638–1715) and replace Britain's old-fashioned parliamentary system with an up-to-date tyranny. In a Protestant nation deeply suspicious of Rome and fiercely protective of its traditional liberties, these turned out to be a recipe for disaster.

In 1688, as tensions between king and Parliament reached the boiling point, William of Orange (1650–1702)—the husband of James's sister Mary and a staunch Protestant—set sail for England with an army. Most of James's own troops refused to fight for him or sided with the invader. In a matter of weeks, James was forced to flee to Ireland, where his remaining forces were crushed at the Battle of the Boyne in 1690.

While most Britons sided with the new regime, a significant minority stayed loyal to the Stuarts, and came to be called Jacobites (after Jacobus, the Latin version of James). It so happened that many leading Jacobites were Freemasons and used their Masonic connections to help recruit allies and further the Stuart cause. As a result, Freemasonry became a battleground between pro- and anti-Stuart factions, and the idea of using Masonic lodges and other secret organizations for political subversion began to spread through European culture.

SEE ALSO: The 'Fifteen (1715), The First Masonic Grand Lodge (1717), The Gormogons (1724), The 'Forty-Five (1745)

A portrait of William III, widely known as William of Orange, painted by Willem Wissing in 1689. In 1688, William played a dramatic and pivotal role in the Glorious Revolution, which brought an end to James II's reign, the last Roman Catholic monarch of England, Scotland, and Ireland. Many of James's supporters, Jacobites, were also Freemasons and loyal to his cause.

Christianity not Mysterious:

OR, A

TREATISE

Shewing,

That there is nothing in the
GOSPEL Contrary to

REASON,

Nor Above it:

And that no Christian Doctrine
can be properly call'd

A MYSTERY.

By *JOHN TOLAND.*

To which is Added,

An Apology for Mr. *Toland,* in rela-
tion to the Parliament of *Ireland's*
ordering this Book to be burnt.

*We need not desire a better Evidence that any Man is in
the wrong, than to hear him declare against Reason, and
thereby to acknowledg that Reason is against him.*
Arch-bishop Tillotson.

London, Printed in the Year 1702.

THE CHEVALIERS OF JUBILATION

JOHN TOLAND (1670–1722) WAS ONE OF THE most controversial authors of a lively age. Born an Irish Catholic, he converted to Protestantism in his teen years, and then veered off in his own direction. His first book, *Christianity Not Mysterious*, rejected the idea that any religion had a monopoly on the truth, and urged that everything in Christianity contrary to reason and common sense should be discarded—a stance that got the book publicly burned in Dublin. Moving to London, he wrote a stream of argumentative essays for the pamphlet press, and soon found it necessary to spend time overseas.

During a stay in the Netherlands between 1708 and 1710, he joined and probably helped found a secret society called the Chevaliers of Jubilation, which met in The Hague. Most of its members were exiles from France and had fled their country because of their opposition to the autocratic rule of King Louis XIV (1638–1715). Their society was partly a drinking club and partly a private joke, but it also functioned as a conspiracy against political and religious conservatism.

The Chevaliers, between drinking bouts, accordingly devoted time to writing propaganda against Louis XIV's regime and smuggling it into France. One of their projects was the most scandalous book of the eighteenth century, *The Treatise on the Three Impostors*, which argued that Moses, Jesus, and Muhammad were swindlers who manufactured fake religions to prey on the gullible, and proposed a new pantheist religion of nature to replace them.

The Chevaliers of Jubilation had little immediate effect on French politics. Over the longer run, though, their efforts helped lay the foundation for the French Revolution, and their methods of subversion through satiric propaganda were adopted by many later secret societies.

SEE ALSO: The French Revolution (1789)

Christianity Not Mysterious was printed in 1702. John Toland, the author of the inflammatory book, helped found the Chevaliers of Jubilation, an underground organization that thrived on bonhomie (lots of drinking) and conspiracy. Although the organization's conspiracy against religious and political conservatism did little to effect change, other secret societies adopted their take on political subversion and made good use of it.

THE 'FIFTEEN

SUPPORTERS OF THE OUSTED HOUSE OF Stuart were jubilant when Queen Anne of Britain (1665–1714) died childless in 1714. They believed that Parliament would have no choice but to invite the son of James II (1633–1701) to assume the British throne as James III (1688–1766). The younger James Stuart was a devout Catholic, and his candidacy was backed by the Vatican and the powerful French King Louis XIV (1638–1715). Many of James's allies thus dreamed of seeing Britain forced back into the Catholic fold—a prospect that most Protestants in Britain regarded with horror.

There was, however, another heir, Prince George of Hanover (1660–1727), a staunch Protestant who was the grandson of James I's daughter Elizabeth. Parliament duly offered him the throne, and George I became the first king of Britain's House of Hanover. Frustrated in his hopes, James Stuart landed in Scotland in 1715 and raised the standard of rebellion. The Jacobite plan depended on their conviction that the common people of Britain would rise up to back them and throw out the Hanoverians, but that belief turned out to be hopelessly mistaken. With little popular support, the rebellion fizzled out, troops loyal to the Hanoverian government closed in, and James and most of his followers had to flee back to France.

The failure of the 1715 rising turned out to have immense consequences for Freemasonry and the wider world of secret societies. Many leading Jacobites were Masons and had used their Masonic connections to recruit allies for their cause. In response, supporters of the Hanoverian cause launched lodges of their own. As the struggle between Stuart and Hanoverian factions moved toward the final explosion in 1745, secret societies came to play a central role in the fight.

SEE ALSO: The Glorious Revolution (1688), The First Masonic Grand Lodge (1717), The 'Forty-Five (1745)

James Stuart, devout Catholic and pretender to the British throne, is shown in this eighteenth-century print, as he sets foot on Scottish soil at Peterhead, on December 22, 1715. His mission was to rally support from other Britains who wished to unseat George I, a staunch Protestant and the first king of Britain's House of Hanover.

THE FIRST MASONIC GRAND LODGE

ACCORDING TO MASONIC HISTORIANS, four lodges of Accepted Masons meeting in London "since time immemorial" agreed in 1717 to form a governing body. Their representatives duly met on June 24 of that year—the feast day of St. John the Baptist, one of the two traditional patrons of the Masonic Craft—at the Apple Tree tavern in London's Covent Garden neighborhood and there founded the Grand Lodge of England, the first grand lodge in the history of Freemasonry.

A complex history lies behind this action. By the first years of the eighteenth century, lodges of Accepted Masons existed in various corners of Scotland and England, some loyal to the exiled House of Stuart, others to the newly installed House of Hanover. The role of Jacobite Freemasons in organizing the 1715 rising did not escape anybody's notice. Once the fighting was over, the Hanoverian faction decided to keep further attempts at subversion in check by creating a grand lodge as a supervisory body for Masonry, with the right to issue and revoke charters for local lodges, under the close supervision of the Hanoverian government.

The founding of the first Grand Lodge went on to have important consequences for the history of Masonry and of secret societies across the Western world, as Masonic grand lodges sprang up in other countries and other organizations quickly adopted the same scheme. It also forced the Jacobites to find ways to evade the watchful eyes of Hanoverian grand lodges—and their efforts kick-started the emergence of a flurry of new Masonic organizations and launched the golden age of secret societies in Europe.

SEE ALSO: The 'Fifteen (1715), The 'Forty-Five (1745).

The Apple Tree Public House as it appears today in London's Covent Garden. Representatives of four ancient lodges of Accepted Masons met at the Apple Tree in 1717, in order to found the first grand lodge in the history of Freemasonry.

A. Chin Quan-Kypo
1st Emperor of China.
The Sage Confucius.
In-Chin present Oecumenical Volgi.-chi
The Mandarin Hang.

From Eastern Climes, transplanted to our Coasts,
Two Oldest Orders, that Creation boasts
Here meet in Miniature, expos'd to view
That by their Conduct, Men may Judge their Due.
The Gormagons, a Venerable Race
Appear Distinguish'd with peculiar Grace.

The Mystery of
Masonry
brought to Light by ye
Gormagons.

What Honour! Wisdom! Truth! & Social Love!
Sure such an Order had its Birth Above.
But Mark Free Masons! what a Farce is this;
How wild their Myst'ry! what a Bum they Kiss
Who would not Laugh when such Occasion's had?
Who should not Weep, to think ye World so Mad.

Done from ye Original,
Painted at Pekin by Mala
chauter, Grav'd by Ho-ge,
and Sold by ye Printsellers
of London Paris & Rome.

Hogarth inv: et Sculp:

THE GORMOGONS

J ACOBITE ATTEMPTS TO SLIP OUT OF THE control of the Hanoverian Grand Lodge of England went in many directions, but few were as colorful as the Ancient Noble Order of Gormogons. This was the brainchild of Philip, Duke of Wharton (1698–1731), one of the few important Jacobites to remain in England after the 1715 uprising. An active Freemason, Wharton became Grand Master of the Grand Lodge in 1722, but stormed out of Masonry the following year. The reason for his abrupt departure was the adoption by the Grand Lodge of the first Book of Constitutions, which required Masons to obey the legal government and closed Masonic lodges to political agitation.

The Order of Gormogons was Wharton's attempt at a rival organization. According to its publicity, the order was founded thousands of years before the time of Adam by Chin-Quaw Ky-Po, the first emperor of China, and had just been brought to England by a Chinese mandarin. It admitted men of all religious and political persuasions, but Freemasons could join only if they renounced Masonry and were expelled from their lodges.

Colorful though the Gormogons' publicity was, the order never attracted more than a few members, though it did manage to become the subject of a famous print by the engraver William Hogarth (1697–1764), one of the great satirical artists of the time. It remained a private project of Wharton's, and when he died in 1731 it quietly dissolved. In the years immediately after Wharton's death, though, similar projects sprouted in Jacobite circles in France. These Jacobite secret societies played a major role in the buildup to the second great Jacobite uprising in 1745.

SEE ALSO: The 'Fifteen (1715), The First Masonic Grand Lodge (1717), Ramsay's Oration (1736), *In Eminente* (1738), The 'Forty-Five (1745).

This print of a William Hogarth engraving, entitled *The Mystery of Masonry Brought to Light by the Gormagons*, illustrates the arrival of the Gormogons in England, led by a Chinese mandarin. It was part of an altogether intriguing but bogus story, which claimed that the Gormogons were founded by Chin-Quaw Ky-Po, the first emperor of China.

RAMSAY'S ORATION

THERE WERE MANY SCOTTISH EXPATRIATES in Europe in the troubled years between the revolution of 1688 and the end of the Jacobite dream at Culloden in 1746. Andrew Ramsay (1686–1743) was one of these; like many others, he became involved in the secret struggle to restore the Stuarts to the British throne. He spent a little over a year as tutor to Charles and Henry Stuart, the heirs of the Stuart line, and remained active in Jacobite circles thereafter.

In 1728, during a brief stay in England, he became a Freemason, and in the years that followed he became active in French Masonic lodges. These were the years when Jacobites and Hanoverians struggled for control over Masonry, and it was also at this same time that Jacobites launched what would later be called the Scottish degrees as a vehicle for their ambitions. Ramsay was in the thick of these intrigues, and was apparently involved in creating the first Scottish degrees and organizing Jacobite Masonry around them.

Certainly Ramsay played a central role in popularizing the new degrees, by way of a famous oration he gave in Paris in 1736 to an audience of distinguished Freemasons. In that oration, he claimed that Freemasonry had descended from the knightly orders of the Crusades—the first time this claim had ever been made publicly. His oration was published in printed form and saw wide distribution. In the short term, it helped Jacobite Masons build the new Scottish degrees into a network of support for the Stuart cause; over the longer term, it inspired countless secret societies to invent romantic origin stories for themselves as a means of publicity.

SEE ALSO: The Glorious Revolution (1688), The First Masonic Grand Lodge (1717), The 'Forty-Five (1745), The Strict Observance (1754)

An eighteenth-century drawing of Andrew Ramsay, who, in 1736, delivered a famous speech in which he claimed that Freemasonry had descended from the knightly orders of the Crusades—the first time this claim had ever been made in public.

IN EMINENTE

NTIL 1738, FREEMASONRY WAS JUST ONE of dozens of little societies, clubs, and social organizations in British society. In that year, a dramatic event set it apart once and for all. Ironically, that event was a denunciation of Freemasonry by the Roman Catholic Church.

In 1738, the Catholic Church was still a major player in European politics. Pope Clement XII (1652–1740) was the absolute ruler of much of central Italy, and his church was a principal support of the authoritarian regimes that dominated most of Europe. Anything from Protestant Britain was suspect in the eyes of Rome, and, as Masonry caught on among European liberals, it became doubly so. Clement accordingly issued a bull (official proclamation), titled *In Eminente* after its opening words, which forbade Catholics from becoming Masons, excommunicated every Catholic who remained a Mason, and reserved the power to forgive them to the pope alone.

The reasons Clement gave for this drastic measure were curiously vague. He cited Masonic secrecy and rumors of Masonic misconduct, but also noted "other just and reasonable motives known to us" which he left entirely unnamed. To this day, no one outside the inner circles of the Vatican knows what those "just and reasonable motives" were.

If Clement hoped to stop the spread of Masonry by the publication of *In Eminente*, he was doomed to disappointment. The reactionary politics backed by the Catholic Church at that time were deeply unpopular among Europe's middle classes, and so the bull succeeded mostly in attracting European liberals to Masonic lodges. The bull also became a serious hindrance for the Jacobite movement, which was busy using Masonry as a cover in its plans for a return to power. Despite this, it remains in force today.

SEE ALSO: The 'Forty-Five (1745)

A portrait of Pope Clement XII, by Agostino Masucci, painted in 1730. In 1738, Pope Clement XII forbade Catholics from becoming Masons in an official proclamation, titled *In Eminente*. Europe's middle classes, however, were so deeply unhappy with the reactionary policies of the Catholic Church that Clement's bull did little to discourage them from joining Masonic lodges.

THE 'FORTY-FIVE

EVERYTHING WAS READY AT LAST. AFTER decades of hard work spreading propaganda, sowing dissension, gathering weapons, and enlisting foreign allies, the great rising that would liberate Britain from the Hanoverian yoke was about to begin. That was what Charles Stuart (1720–1788)—the "Bonnie Prince Charlie" of Scottish legend—and his followers believed, as they boarded ships to sail from Brittany to Scotland to raise the flag of revolt in 1745.

As it turned out, the Jacobites had simply repeated the mistakes of 1715 on a larger scale. Most people in Britain regarded the Stuart cause with suspicion because of its alliance with the Catholic Church and the French. Many of the Scottish Highland clans rallied to Charles's banner, and Stuart rebels seized Edinburgh, defeated several small British forces, and marched south as far as Derby, but the great rising never happened. As the British Army closed in, the rebels retreated to Scotland, where they suffered a catastrophic defeat in 1746 at Culloden.

"The 'Forty-Five," as it came to be known in Scottish legend, was the last gasp of the Jacobite cause. Charles Stuart returned to exile in France and then in Rome, where he died a bitter alcoholic in 1788. The secret societies that had funneled arms and money to the rebellion were pressed into service to help defeated Jacobites flee to safety abroad. In the decades that followed, Scottish Masonry and several other Jacobite branches of Freemasonry gave up politics for other missions. Meanwhile, the secret society methods that had been developed in the long struggle between Stuarts and Hanoverians found new uses as radicals began to take aim at the conservative monarchs of Europe.

SEE ALSO: The 'Fifteen (1715), The Strict Observance (1754)

1745

David Morier's 1746 painting of *The Battle of Culloden*, vividly depicts the defeat of Charles Stuart's ("Bonnie Prince Charlie's") supporters by the British in 1746. After Stuart sailed to Scotland to raise the flag of revolt in 1745, his last hope of liberating Britain from the Hanoverian regime was completely extinguished at Culloden.

THE HELL-FIRE CLUB

THE SAME DUKE OF WHARTON (1698–1731) who founded the Gormogons in 1724 had briefly launched another, even more colorful secret society back in 1719. The Hell-Fire Club lasted barely a year before it went into abeyance, but it rose again in the wake of the 1745 rebellion when a dissident aristocrat as colorful as Wharton—Sir Francis Dashwood (1708–1781)—revived it.

Dashwood was a friend of the colorful Lady Mary Wortley Montagu (1689–1762), who had been Wharton's mistress in the days of the original club and participated in its rites. He and a group of roistering friends began meeting in rented rooms at a London pub, the George and Vulture, while Dashwood had a medieval abbey at Medmenham remodeled as the club's permanent base. Once Medmenham Abbey was restored to its original splendor, and immense supplies of liquor and a world-class collection of pornography had been brought in, members of the club went there for regular meetings and ceremonies.

The ceremonies were classic expressions of the Gothic taste of the time. Members dressed in black hooded robes and took part in burlesque pseudo-Satanic rites, accompanied by scantily clad "nuns" who were either noblewomen of easy virtue or prostitutes hired for the weekend. Astonishing amounts of liquor were consumed in these celebrations, which inevitably ended with an orgy. All this was typical behavior among the English upper class of the time, but some historians have argued that the Hell-Fire Club also served a serious purpose, as a center for Jacobite propaganda and of opposition to the existing order of British society. It also helped feed popular notions of secret societies as centers of debauchery and deviance.

SEE ALSO: The Chevaliers of Jubilation (c. 1710), The Gormogons (1724), The 'Forty-Five (1745), The "Palladian Order" Hoax (1897)

William Hogarth's portrait of Sir Francis Dashwood, painted c. 1764, brilliantly parodies Renaissance images of Francis of Assisi; it shows Dashwood at his devotions, wearing a habit, and adoring a naked Venus in place of a crucifix. The scene perfectly expresses the colorful environment of the Hell-Fire Club, originally founded by the Duke of Wharton (of Gormogon fame) in 1719 and subsequently reinvented by Sir Francis Dashwood in 1745.

THE ANCIENT-MODERN SCHISM

THE TOTAL DEFEAT OF BONNIE PRINCE Charlie's Jacobite forces at Culloden in 1746 ended the last hope of a Jacobite restoration in England, but it did nothing to bridge the bitter divides that the long era of Jacobite–Hanoverian feuding had brought to Freemasonry. If anything, the end of the fighting hardened those divisions, and a split became inevitable.

In 1751, accordingly, a group of Jacobite Freemasons of Irish descent living in London formed their own Grand Lodge, calling it the Ancient or Antient Grand Lodge (both spellings were then in common use), and proclaiming that the existing Grand Lodge had abandoned the traditions of Masonry. The original Grand Lodge of England, which was loyal to the House of Hanover, thus came to be called the Modern Grand Lodge. A number of existing lodges left the Modern Grand Lodge and joined the Ancients, and the Ancient Grand Lodge organized other lodges.

For more than sixty years thereafter, England had two feuding Masonic Grand Lodges, and members of lodges under each jurisdiction were strictly forbidden from attending meetings of lodges of the other.

The split did not resolve until 1815, when everyone who had taken sides in the long quarrel between Jacobites and Hanoverians was safely dead. In that year, the two Grand Lodges finally joined forces to become the United Grand Lodge of England. Across the Atlantic, similar unions brought together competing Grand Lodges in many states of the Union. The one remaining vestige of the old quarrel is that, to this day, some Grand Lodges in the United States append the initials F. & A.M. (Free and Accepted Masons) to their titles, while others use A.F. & A.M. (Ancient Free and Accepted Masons).

SEE ALSO: The 'Forty-Five (1745)

A photograph of the present United Grand Lodge of England, Freemason's Hall in London, built between 1927 and 1932. Freemasons have met on the site for more than two centuries.

THE STRICT OBSERVANCE

BARON KARL GOTTHELF VON HUND (1722–1776) was a man with a mission. In 1743, shortly after he was first initiated into Freemasonry, he went to Paris and there received from the Jacobite Earl of Kilmarnock a set of secret degrees that claimed to date from the original Knights Templar. For the next eleven years, he kept his vows of secrecy strictly. In 1754, though, he was called back to Paris and there received permission to make the Templar degrees public. On his return to Saxony, he launched a new order of Templar Masonry called the Rite of Strict Observance.

For the next twenty years, the Strict Observance flourished in central Europe, attracting members from other Masonic rites. Von Hund claimed that the Strict Observance was part of a much larger and more secret body, headed by Bonnie Prince Charlie, whose Unknown Superiors were prepared to pass on the secrets of alchemy and the location of buried Templar treasures.

These promises understandably attracted a great deal of interest, and they inspired the rise of a rival order, the Golden and Rosy Cross, with its own claims to possession of alchemical secrets.

Unfortunately for von Hund, the Unknown Superiors never followed through on their promises. He never seems to have realized that the entire structure of Templar Masonry was born as a vehicle for Jacobite political ambitions, and the failure of the Jacobite cause to recover from the disaster at Culloden meant that his efforts had no further value for the Stuarts and their allies. At the Convention of Wilhelmsbad in 1782, six years after von Hund's death, the order dissolved and members went into a variety of other secret societies.

SEE ALSO: The 'Forty-Five (1745), The Golden and Rosy Cross (1755), The Convention of Wilhelmsbad (1782)

Baron Karl Gotthelf von Hund, in a contemporary painting. The Strict Observance, established by Hund in 1754, enjoyed a fair amount of popularity initially, but the order eventually petered out by 1782. Hund died in 1776, en route to a meeting with the reigning Duke Friedrich August, whom he hoped to convince to adopt the Strict Observance.

MYSTERIVM MAGNVM STVDIVM VNIVERSALI.

TINCTURA

alba.

TINCTURA

rubra

LIE   BE.

MAGISTER IESUS CHRISTUS

D. et H.

Das ist das guldene Rosen
Bruder von feinem Golde

Creutz, welches ein jeder
auf seiner Brust trägt.

Benedictus
Dominus Deus Noster,
qui dedit nobis
Signum.

GLAUBE.   HOFFNUNG.

Frater
Roseæ et Aureæ
Crucis

GED   ULT.

TINCTUR.

Höre mein Kind, und nimm an meine
Rede, damit deine Jahre vermehret werden,
Ich will dir den Weg der Weißheit zeigen,
und dich führen durch die Bahn der Gerechtig-
keit. Wenn du darauf gehen wirst, so sollen
dir deine Gänge nicht beängstiget werden, und
wann du geschwinde lauffest, wirst du nicht an-
stoßen. Halte die Lehre, und bewahre
sie, denn sie ist dein Leben. Prov. IV. v. 10.

Die Lehre Jesu Christi übertrifft die
Lehre aller Heiligen, und die Brüder, die den
Geist Gottes haben, finden darinnen das ver-
borgene Himmel-Brod, und den Stein der
Weisen, ☿. ♃. ☉. Es geschiehet aber, daß
viele Menschen, ob sie schon oft das Evange-
lium und die Sprache der Weisen hören, jedoch
keine Begierde daraus empfinden, denn sie haben den Geist Christi nicht. Wer aber die
Worte Christi verstehen will, und der Weisen
Reden ergründen, der muß sich befleißigen, mit
seinem Leben Christo gleichförmig zu werden.

Ich will dir grosse und gewaltige Dinge zeigen.
Jerem. XXXIII.

THE GOLDEN AND ROSY CROSS

THE RISE OF THE STRICT OBSERVANCE troubled European Freemasons of conservative leanings, who recognized its connections with the Jacobite movement and worried (with good reason) that the Jacobite experience might inspire attempts to overthrow other governments. The obvious response was a competing secret society, and Hermann Fichtuld (c. 1700–1777), a Freemason and occultist, duly founded one. Since the Strict Observance had already staked a claim to the Knights Templar, Fichtuld's new order claimed the legacy of the one legendary organization as romantic as the Templars—the original Rosicrucians.

The Order of the Golden and Rosy Cross was an immediate success, not least because it offered its members an extensive study course in occultism and alchemy. Members had to pass an examination in the symbolism of each degree and in a substantial body of esoteric teachings before passing to the next degree. By the 1770s, the order had several thousand members throughout central Europe; in the following decade, it carried on a lively feud with the Bavarian Illuminati and a splinter group founded by some of its own ex-members, the Asiatic Brethren.

In 1786, one of its members ascended the throne of Prussia as King Friedrich Wilhelm II (1744–1797), and appointed several other leading members to high political office. For the next ten years, the Golden and Rosy Cross was quite literally the power behind the throne in Prussia, the most powerful of the small kingdoms into which Germany was still divided. Friedrich Wilhelm's death in 1797, though, robbed the order of its power base, and the cataclysm of the Napoleonic Wars in the decades immediately afterward shattered what remained.

SEE ALSO: The Rosicrucians (1614), The Strict Observance (1754), The Bavarian Illuminati (1776)

An image from *Geheime Figuren der Rosenkreuzer, aus dem 16ten und 17ten Jarhundert* (Secret symbols of the Rosicrucians from the sixteenth and seventeenth centuries), an eighteenth-century document that has been reprinted countless times.

Fraunces Tavern, NEW YORK.

THE COMMITTEES OF CORRESPONDENCE

CONSPIRACY RESEARCHERS HAVE GENERALLY neglected the American Revolution, preferring to focus attention on more glamorous European events such as the French and Russian Revolutions. This is ironic, because it is well documented that the American Revolution was launched by at least two conspiracies, the Committees of Correspondence and the Sons of Liberty.

The Committees of Correspondence began to organize themselves around 1760 as the interests of American colonists and the British government came more and more into conflict. Their members were drawn from leading citizens in the colonies, and they focused at first on circulating news and lobbying the government in London for reforms. As tensions rose and positions hardened, the Committees of Correspondence shifted the focus of their activities to organizing campaigns of civil disobedience against the British government, and then to preparing for the war that was certain to break out.

Many of the leading members of the Committees of Correspondence were also Freemasons. While there is no evidence for any formal link between colonial Masonic lodges and the Committees, the Committees doubtless used Masonic connections to recruit members.

In 1765, the Committees in New York and Boston played a central role in helping to found the other major secret society of the American Revolution, the Sons of Liberty. In 1773, as British troops flooded the colonies, the Committees merged their operations with the legislatures of the colonies, helping to found the Continental Congress in 1776. Many members of the Committees of Correspondence went on to become members of the Continental Congress and played leading roles in the Revolution, while the Committees themselves quietly dissolved.

SEE ALSO: The Sons of Liberty (1765)

Fraunces Tavern, situated at 54 Pearl Street at the corner of Broad Street in lower Manhattan. The tavern became a haven and meeting place in the early 1760s for organizations such as the Committees of Correspondence, which played a central role in founding the Sons of Liberty (1765).

The BLOODY MASSACRE perpetrated in King—Street BOSTON on March 5th 1770 by a party of the 29th REGt.

Engrav'd Printed & Sold by PAUL REVERE BOSTON

BUTCHER'S HALL

Unhappy BOSTON! see thy Sons deplore,
Thy hallow'd Walks besmear'd with guiltless Gore.
While faithless P—n and his savage Bands,
With murd'rous Rancour stretch their bloody Hands;
Like fierce Barbarians grinning o'er their Prey,
Approve the Carnage, and enjoy the Day.

If scalding drops from Rage from Anguish Wrung
If speechless Sorrows lab'ring for a Tongue,
Or if a weeping World can ought appease
The plaintive Ghosts of Victims such as these:
The Patriot's copious Tears for each are shed,
A glorious Tribute which embalms the Dead.

But know, FATE summons to that awful Goal,
Where JUSTICE strips the Murd'rer of his Soul:
Should venal C—ts the scandal of the Land,
Snatch the relentless Villain from her Hand,
Keen Execrations on this Plate inscrib'd,
Shall reach a JUDGE who never can be brib'd.

The unhappy Sufferers were Messrs SAML GRAY, SAML MAVERICK, JAMS CALDWELL, CRISPUS ATTUCKS & PATK CARR
Killed. Six wounded; two of them (CHRISTR MONK & JOHN CLARK) Mortally

Published in 1770 by Paul Revere Boston

THE SONS OF LIBERTY

FOR MOST OF A DECADE BEFORE 1765, RELA-tions between the British government and the people of the thirteen British colonies came under increasing strain. The colonists thought of themselves as British subjects, with the same rights as their peers across the sea; the government saw them as cash cows to be milked dry for London's benefit. When Parliament passed the Stamp Act, levying expensive taxes on the colonists, an explosion became inevitable.

One colonial conspiracy already existed—the Committees of Correspondence—but it drew its membership from among the wealthy and influential, and focused on lobbying and political organization. A new secret Society, the Sons of Liberty, promptly emerged to pursue the same goal by more robust means. Organized in 1765 in New York and Boston, it fought the Stamp Act and other edicts from London with a mix of civil disobedience and rioting.

The Boston Massacre of 1770, when British troops stationed in Boston fired into a crowd and killed five civilians, convinced many colonists that armed resistance was their only option. The Sons of Liberty began gathering guns and ammunition. A rising spiral of violence on both sides culminated on the night of April 17–18, 1775, when British soldiers marched out of Boston to seize Sons of Liberty arsenals in surrounding towns.

Paul Revere (1734–1818), a leading member of the Sons of Liberty, made his famous midnight ride to warn fellow members of the raid. The organization's paramilitary branch, the Minutemen, turned out in force, and the battles of Lexington and Concord took place the next morning. The American Revolution was on.

SEE ALSO: The Committees of Correspondence (1760)

An engraving by Paul Revere, published by Revere in 1770, depicts the Boston Massacre (1770), a harrowing event and flashpoint for the American Revolution, after five civilians were killed by British troops. An armed revolt, organized by the Sons of Liberty—with Paul Revere playing a leading role—was leveled against the British in April 1775.

DICTIONNAIRE

MYTHO-HERMÉTIQUE,

DANS LEQUEL ON TROUVE

Les Allégories Fabuleuses des Poetes, les Métaphores, les Énigmes et les Termes barbares des Philosophes Hermétiques expliqués.

Par Dom Antoine-Joseph Pernety, *Religieux Bénédictin de la Congrégation de Saint-Maur.*

Sapiens animadvertet parabolam & interpretationem, verba sapientum, & ænigmata eorum. Prov. 1. v. 6.

Remi *Pierret...*

A PARIS, *Quai des Augustins.*

Chez BAUCHE, Libraire, à Sainte Genevieve & à S. Jean dans le Désert.

M. DCC. LVIII.

AVEC APPROBATION ET PRIVILEGE DU ROI.

THE ILLUMINÉS OF AVIGNON

FRANCE BEFORE THE REVOLUTION WAS FULL of mystics, occultists, and visionaries of all kinds, and the hothouse atmosphere of eighteenth-century Freemasonry encouraged many of them to launch Masonic and quasi-Masonic organizations to spread their teachings. Antoine-Joseph Pernety (1716–1796) was one of these. Originally a Catholic—he spent several years as a Benedictine monk—he converted to the mystical Christianity of the Swedish mystic Emanuel Swedenborg (1688–1772). Sometime in the 1760s, he became a Freemason and convinced himself that Swedenborg's teachings were actually the inner secrets of Freemasonry.

In 1770 he founded a new Masonic order in the French town of Avignon, where he then lived. Named the Illuminés of Avignon, this order used the three degrees of ordinary Masonry and added to it a fourth degree titled *True Mason*, which passed on the Swedenborgian teachings to initiates. The new organization was a modest success, but in 1778 it suddenly changed its name to the Academy of True Masons. The reason for this change may well have been the birth in 1776 of a very different order with a similar name—the Bavarian Illuminati.

Conspiracy researchers have claimed for many years that the Illuminés of Avignon, like the Alumbrados before them, were somehow identical to the Bavarian Illuminati. In fact, the similarity stops with the name; it's hard to think of two things with less in common than Pernety's gentle Swedenborgian Christianity and the rationalist radicalism of Adam Weishaupt (1748–1830). Yet these two very different organizations turned out to share a common fate: both of them went out of existence as Europe descended into chaos after the French Revolution.

SEE ALSO: The Alumbrados (1511), The Bavarian Illuminati (1776)

The front cover of **Dictionnaire Mytho-Hermétique** (Mytho-hermetic dictionary), published by Antoine-Joseph Pernety in 1778. Influenced by the Christian mysticism of Emanuel Swedenborg. Pernety founded a new Masonic order in Avignon, France, in 1770. The book cast light on the mysterious inner workings of Freemasonry.

Adam Weishaupt.

geb. d. 6. Febr. 1748.

THE BAVARIAN ILLUMINATI

THE MOST FAMOUS CONSPIRACY OF THEM all, the focus of more than two hundred years of rumor and terror, the Bavarian Illuminati started out as a college club. Adam Weishaupt (1748–1830), its founder, was a professor of law at Ingolstadt University in Bavaria, and on May 1, 1776, he and four friends organized a club to discuss the exciting new liberal ideas then being discussed in France. As the club attracted new members, Weishaupt invented initiation rituals, drew up a study course to spread these same ideas among new initiates, and focused on recruiting members among the wealthy, the talented, and the socially prominent.

As his ambitions grew, he came to see the Illuminati as an elite of enlightened, rational individuals who would insinuate themselves into key positions in Bavarian society and turn the country into a utopia. Illuminati accordingly began to infiltrate Masonic lodges and make connections with political radicals in France and elsewhere. While the Illuminati failed in their attempt to seize control of the Strict Observance in 1782, their star was rising.

Unfortunately for Weishaupt's dreams, Bavaria in the late eighteenth century was a deeply conservative Catholic nation whose royal court was profoundly suspicious of the new ideas from France. Rumors of the order's activities and agenda began to spread as members talked too freely, and the inevitable backlash came. Laws passed in 1784 and 1785 banned the Illuminati, and a series of police raids broke the back of the organization and seized hundreds of pages of documents. Weishaupt fled the country; many other members of the order were less lucky and spent long terms in Bavarian prisons.

SEE ALSO: The Strict Observance (1754), The Convention of Wilhelmsbad (1782), The French Revolution (1789), The Social Circle (1790), *Proofs of a Conspiracy* (1797)

Johan Adam Weishaupt, pictured in a 1799 engraving. In 1776, Weishaupt, a professor of law at Ingolstadt University in Bavaria, founded the Illuminati. Ultimately, Weishaupt's aim was to turn Bavaria into a utopia.

THE CONVENTION OF WILHELMSBAD

BEFORE EUROPE DESCENDED INTO THE chaos of the Napoleonic Wars, Wilhelmsbad was a popular resort town in what is now Germany. That was why Duke Ferdinand of Brunswick (1721–1792), Grand Master of the Order of Strict Observance, summoned members of his order there in the summer of 1782, and invited members of other Masonic rites to join in the deliberations. The Convention's purpose was to sort out the claims made by the order's founder, Baron von Hund (1722–1776), about Masonry's links to the Knights Templar and to the secrets of occultism.

The Strict Observance, the largest Masonic rite in Europe at that time, was in crisis, because von Hund's promises of secret wisdom forthcoming from the order's Unknown Superiors had never been kept. The Bavarian Illuminati, then busy infiltrating Masonic lodges all over Europe, thus sent members to the Convention to try to seize control of what was left of the Strict Observance and turn it into a vehicle for the Illuminati program of radical rationalism. On the other side was a cadre of Masons led by Jean-Baptiste Willermoz (1730–1824), who wanted to see European Masonry return to charitable and fraternal purposes.

When the Convention closed after thirty sessions, Willermoz and his allies had won. The attendees agreed that there was no evidence for Templar origin for Masonry; and a new ritual, the degree of Beneficent Knights of the Holy City, was penned by Willermoz and adopted by many lodges that had been part of the Strict Observance. The Illuminati returned to Bavaria with few recruits to show for their pains. In the Convention's wake, European Freemasonry followed the British model, and political conspirators and occultists began to found new orders for their own purposes outside Masonry.

SEE ALSO: The Strict Observance (1754), The Bavarian Illuminati (1776)

A contemporary photo of Wilhelmsbad Castle, now in ruins. In the summer of 1782, Duke Ferdinand of Brunswick, Grand Master of the Order of Strict Observance, summoned members of his order to Wilhelmsbad to put to rest the widely held claim that Masonry originated with the Knights Templar.

THE FRENCH REVOLUTION

SOME REVOLUTIONS BEGIN WITH GUNFIRE and explosions, but the French Revolution began with a vote. On June 17, 1789, the lower house of the États Généraux, the rarely convened parliament of France, declared itself the National Assembly and took control of the troubled kingdom. In July, a mob sacked the Bastille; in October, the king and queen became prisoners of the new regime; laws passed over the months that followed stripped the aristocracy and the Catholic Church of their traditional privileges. In a few short months, a system of government that had been in place for a millennium vanished forever.

Perceptive observers had realized for years that France was stumbling toward convulsive change. The French government was an economic basket case propped up by immense deficits, and the monarchy had lost the respect of the people. In the turmoil that followed the Revolution, though, many people went looking for scapegoats. The furor surrounding the Bavarian Illuminati was only a few years in the past, and so secret societies were an obvious target. Rumors soon spread throughout Europe, blaming the Revolution on this or that conspiracy.

The claims that secret societies had stage-managed the French Revolution had an unexpected result: in the decades following the Revolution, people of every political allegiance who wanted to bring about change listened to these claims, decided to give conspiracy a try, and founded secret societies to pursue their goals. The French Revolution thus became a seedbed of secret societies, and launched a golden age of political conspiracy across the Western world.

SEE ALSO: The Bavarian Illuminati (1776), The Social Circle (1790), The Conspiracy of Equals (1796), The Philadelphes (1797), Proofs of a Conspiracy (1797), The Carbonari (1800), The Sublime Perfect Masters (1809), The Chevaliers of Faith (1810)

The 1789 attack on the Bastille, depicted in an eighteenth-century lithograph. The Bastille was a state prison and symbol of the monarchy's oppressive rule. The morning after the attack, the king, Louis XVI (1754–1793), asked the Duke of La Rochefoucauld, "Is it a revolt?" The duke answered, "No sire, it's not a revolt; it's a revolution."

BONAPARTE AT ARCOLE.

FROM THE PAINTING IN THE LOUVRE BY ANTOINE-JEAN GROS. THIS PORTRAIT WAS PAINTED BY GROS IN ITALY IN 1797; AT THE SOLICITATION
OF JOSEPHINE, BONAPARTE SAT FOR IT. IT WAS PRESENTED TO THE LOUVRE IN 1883 BY Mme MILLIET. IT IS NOT THE PAINTING FROM WHICH THE
LONGHI ENGRAVING WAS MADE, BUT MOST PROBABLY THE SKETCH MADE FROM LIFE FOR THE PAINTING.

THE SOCIAL CIRCLE

A S THE NEW NATIONAL ASSEMBLY TIGHT-ened its control over revolutionary France, power struggles between moderates and radicals accelerated. Nicholas de Bonneville (1760–1828) was one of the radicals. A member of the Social Club, the radical faction headed by Philippe d'Orléans, he also had close connections with the Bavarian Illuminati in Germany. He was the logical person to found one of the most influential secret societies of the early revolutionary period. The Social Circle, the organization he founded to advance the radical agenda, quickly recruited thousands of fellow radicals and began to exert pressure on the National Assembly, pushing for such then-unthinkable ideas as equal rights for women and a social-welfare system.

Like most political secret societies before and since, the Social Circle walked a fine line between secrecy and publicity. Its members kept their identities secret, but the Circle publicized itself through a newspaper, *Le Bouche de Fer* (The mouth of iron), and a front organization, The Universal Confederation of the Friends of Truth. While its headquarters stayed in Paris and French politics remained its central focus, it had branches in London, Utrecht, Geneva, Genoa, and across the Atlantic in Philadelphia.

In 1799, the hopes of the radicals were dashed when an army officer named Napoleon Bonaparte (1769–1821) staged a coup of his own and took control of France. The Social Circle went out of existence thereafter, but many of its members ended up in secret societies such as the Conspiracy of Equals and the Philadelphes, which set out to launch a second French Revolution to overthrow Napoleon's regime.

SEE ALSO: The Bavarian Illuminati (1776), The Conspiracy of Equals (1796), The Philadelphes (1797)

Radical organizations like the Social Circle sprang up in France after the revolution, hoping to advance a socially progressive agenda. Their plans were derailed when Napoleon Bonaparte, seen here in a 1796 painting by Antoine-Jean Gros, staged a coup of his own.

THE LOYAL ORANGE ORDER

IRELAND IN THE 1790S WAS A SEETHING CAUL-dron of sectarian hatred. A Protestant minority backed by Britain's colonial rule dominated the Catholic majority, and violence on both sides was an everyday occurrence. There had been plenty of secret societies in Ireland before then, Protestant as well as Catholic, but when Britain's Parliament passed the Catholic Relief Act in 1793, threatening the privileged status of the Protestant minority, the most notorious of the Protestant secret societies was born: the Loyal Orange Order.

The Orange Order took its name from William of Orange (1650–1702), whose victory over the Stuart king James II (1633–1701), at the Battle of the Boyne in 1690, had cemented Protestant rule over Ireland. Like many political secret societies of the time, this order had a public and a covert face. The public face used legal and generally peaceful means to pressure the British government to maintain Protestant privileges in Ireland; the covert face used intimidation, violence, and terrorism to pursue the same goals. The order's leadership publicly disavowed violence while covertly encouraging it, and used the threat of terrorism as a bargaining chip in negotiations with the British colonial government.

The Orange Order spread rapidly among Irish Protestants and played a major role in the troubled politics of British-ruled Ireland all the way until Ireland won its independence in 1921. Thereafter, its only remaining lodges on the Emerald Isle were in Northern Ireland, which remained under British rule. It played a massive role in the sectarian violence in Northern Ireland during the second half of the twentieth century, and it also has a substantial presence today in Scotland, Canada, and a few other countries.

SEE ALSO: The Glorious Revolution (1688), The Easter Rising (1916)

The Loyal Orange Order was named after William of Orange, seen in this striking 1695 portrait by Godfried Schalcken (1643–1706), where William is shown lit only by a candle. William's defeat of the deposed King James II at the Battle of Boyne in 1690 ensured Protestant ascendancy in Ireland.

Constitution
de 1795.
l'An 3.

CONJURATION DE BABOEUF L'AN IV.

La France sous la forme d'une Mère nourice jeune et vigoureuse admire l'harmonie de sa Constitution, des Authorités établies, et des Départemens. l'Anarchie furieuse et jalouse, conseillée par un Serpent astutieux va plonger ses poignards dans le sein de la Patrie. Mais le Génie deffenseur de la République, l'arrête dans ses fureurs.

THE CONSPIRACY OF EQUALS

FRANÇOIS "GRACCHUS" BABEUF (1760–1797) and Filippo Buonarroti (1761–1837) were already seasoned radicals when they met in prison in 1795. Both men had supported the Jacobins, the radical party that pushed the French Revolution to its brutal extreme, and both landed in jail once the Jacobins were overthrown and the more conservative Directory took control of France. Babeuf had been a close associate of Nicholas de Bonneville (1760–1828), founder of the Social Circle, and he and Buonarroti laid plans to found another political conspiracy along the same lines as soon as they got out of prison.

Their chance came in November 1795, when they were released. They immediately founded an organization called the Society of the Pantheon, borrowing most of the details from the Social Circle. When the Directory ordered the Society suppressed in February 1796, Babeuf and Buonarroti immediately founded a more secret organization, the Conspiracy of Equals, and began recruiting government and military personnel. Where older revolutionary secret societies tried to spark the same kind of mass movement that overthrew the French monarchy, the Conspiracy of Equals aimed at a coup d'état led by a small force of committed revolutionaries.

Unfortunately for their plans, the Directory had planted an informer in their ranks and struck first, arresting some 200 members. Babeuf was executed, but Buonarroti survived to become the most influential founder of political secret societies in the first half of the nineteenth century. The plan of seizing power through a coup d'état also spread widely, and gave the Bolsheviks in 1917 and the Nazis in 1933 their basic strategy.

SEE ALSO: The Social Circle (1790), The Russian Revolution (1917), Hitler Takes Power (1933)

The Conspiracy of Equals (1796), is belittled in this 1796 engraving. The coup, led by François-Noël Babeuf, known as Gracchus Babeuf, failed during the French Revolutionary period.

THE BLACK LEAGUE

THE FRENCH REVOLUTION DID NOT STAY confined to France for long. In the aftermath of the National Assembly's seizure of power, several other European nations sent troops to try to restore the deposed Bourbon kings to power. The revolutionary government in France responded by raising huge armies and fighting the invaders to a standstill, then launched a successful invasion of Italy in 1795. French armies overwhelmed the little half-medieval states of Italy and established puppet governments to run a set of newly invented nations.

The publicity surrounding the Bavarian Illuminati a few years before the French invasion guaranteed that Italians opposed to the new state of affairs would turn to conspiracy. The first such group was the Lega Nera, or Black League, founded around 1796 in northern Italy. Little is known about the Lega Nera, outside reports on its activities that survive in the archives of the French secret police. According to these sources, the Black League was connected to the same radical Jacobin circles in Paris that created the Social Circle and later spawned the Conspiracy of Equals, and planned a campaign of assassination aimed at French officials and military officers.

The planned campaign never happened, but the rise of the Black League was still an event of immense importance in the history of conspiracies. For a century after the French invasion, Italy would be a hotbed of revolutionary secret societies, and some of the largest and most influential of those groups—the Philadelphes, the Carbonari, and the Sublime Perfect Masters—would have influence far outside Italy's borders.

SEE ALSO: The Conspiracy of Equals (1796), The Philadelphes (1797), The Raggi (1797), The Carbonari (1800), The Sublime Perfect Masters (1809)

An illustration of Napoleon Bonaparte (1769–1821) and his staff, c. 1796, during the successful Italian Campaigns (1792-1802). The Black League's plans to assassinate French military officers never came to fruition as Napoleon's victories swept over Italy.

THE PHILADELPHES

IN THE HOTHOUSE ENVIRONMENT OF REVOLU-tionary France, as secret societies sprang up like mushrooms after a spring rain, organizations founded for completely different purposes got drawn into the whirlpool of political conspiracy. That's what happened to the Philadelphes. Founded by college students in Besançon in eastern France as a literary club—the name comes from the Greek words for "brotherly love"—it got into politics after Napoleon seized power in 1799, and mutated into a full-blown conspiracy in the years that followed. Though it managed to infiltrate six French Army regiments, it never managed to spark a popular uprising.

The Philadelphes spread to Italy and Switzerland after 1807, when a group of Italian exiles in Paris were initiated into it. After Napoleon's regime finally ended in 1815, the order became committed to agitation for constitutional government in France and Italy, and was heavily involved in the devious politics of the radical underground in those years. For a while it was infiltrated by another secret society with similar aims, the Sublime Perfect Masters, and it took part in preparations for the widespread European rebellions of 1820 and 1821.

Thereafter, as revolutionary organizations abandoned the secret society model and formed political parties instead, the Philadelphes became an anachronism in the European radical scene. When Napoleon's nephew staged a coup d'état in France in 1852 and proclaimed himself Napoleon III, though, French exiles in London revived it, and proceeded to use it as a front organization to launch the First International—the first major Communist organization. In the conflicts that surrounded the First International's rise and fall, the Philadelphe order went quietly out of existence.

SEE ALSO: The Sublime Perfect Masters (1809), The First International (1864)

A contemporary view of Besançon, France, where a group of college students founded the Philadelphes. Originally a literary club, the organization morphed into a powerful political entity after Napoleon's rise to power in 1799.

THE RAGGI

WHILE THE FIRST MEMBERS OF THE Philadelphes were meeting to read poetry in Besançon, a political secret society at least as influential was taking shape in northern Italy. The French invasion of Italy in 1795 was welcomed at first by Italian political radicals, who welcomed an end to the reactionary governments under which they lived. When the newly founded Cisalpine Republic turned out to be a puppet state that took orders from Paris, and attempts by the radicals to win self-government by peaceful means met with violent reprisals, the Raggi was born.

The Italian word *raggi* means "rays." Each member of the organization was part of a group of five, a *ray*, which had no contact with other rays. One member of the ray reported to a member of a *segment*, the regional coordinating body, and each segment reported to one of two independent *hemispheres*, which reported to the supreme body, the *solar circle*. This system of organization made it difficult for the secret police to locate and arrest more than a few members of the organization at a time.

The Raggi itself achieved little directly. While it reached a total membership between 30,000 and 50,000 at its peak in 1804, it came under increasing pressure from the French-backed regime on the one hand and local conservatives on the other. After Napoleon's defeat, when the old reactionary governments were reestablished with the backing of the Austrian army, the Raggi went out of existence and most of its active members joined the Carbonari and the Philadelphes. The system of organization pioneered by the Raggi, though, went on to become standard practice in revolutionary secret societies across Europe.

SEE ALSO: The Philadelphes (1797), The Carbonari (1800)

Entry of the French Army in Rome **(1797),** a painting by Hippolyte Lecomte (1781–1857), depicts the initial enthusiasm for the French incursion into Italy. When it became clear that the new, and increasingly violent, regime took its orders from Paris, disgruntlement set it in, and secret, decentralized resistance organizations like the Raggi sprang up.

PROOFS

OF A

CONSPIRACY

AGAINST ALL THE

RELIGIONS AND GOVERNMENTS

OF

EUROPE,

CARRIED ON

IN THE SECRET MEETINGS

OF

FREE MASONS, ILLUMINATI,

AND

READING SOCIETIES.

COLLECTED FROM GOOD AUTHORITIES,

By JOHN ROBISON, A. M.

PROFESSOR OF NATURAL PHILOSOPHY, AND SECRETARY TO THE
ROYAL SOCIETY OF EDINBURGH.

Nam tua res agitur paries cum proximus ardet.

The THIRD EDITION.

To which is added a POSTSCRIPT.

———————

PHILADELPHIA:

PRINTED FOR T. DOBSON, N°. 41, SOUTH SECOND
STREET, AND W. COBBET, N°. 25, NORTH
SECOND STREET.
1798.

PROOFS OF A CONSPIRACY

By 1797, RUMORS BLAMING THE FRENCH Revolution on various sinister conspiracies had reached fever pitch. That was the year when a Scottish author named John Robison (1739–1805) published a book entitled *Proofs of a Conspiracy against All the Religions and Governments of Europe, Carried on in the Secret Meetings of Free Masons, Illuminati and Reading Societies*. In it, Robison claimed that the Bavarian Illuminati had infiltrated European Freemasonry as a platform to launch revolutions against every European government and church.

Robison wasn't the only author making such claims at that time. A French author, Augustin de Barruel (1741–1820), published in the same year the first two volumes of a lengthy treatise making similar claims, and Charles-Louis Cadet de Gassicourt (1769–1821) had beaten both of them to the punch the previous year with a lurid book, *The Tomb of Jacques de Molay*, which insisted that the Masons had overthrown the French monarchy to avenge the destruction of the Knights Templar. Yet it was Robison's book, far more than the other two, that was studied and reprinted by conspiracy researchers from then on.

Ironically, Robison was a Freemason, and hoped to use the bad example of European Freemasonry to persuade his fellow Masons in Britain to keep their lodges out of politics. His book, though, was used for two centuries thereafter to insist that all Masonic lodges were sinister political conspiracies.

SEE ALSO: Fall of the Knights Templar (1307), The Bavarian Illuminati (1776), The French Revolution (1789)

Title page of John Robison's book, *Proofs of Conspiracy*, published in 1798. Robison's exposé of the stealthy, mysterious, and, as some would have it, diabolical schemes of the Illuminati, Freemasons, and other secret societies, created a sensation in Europe and America.

THE CARBONARI

O F ALL THE SECRET SOCIETIES TO COME out of the Napoleonic era, the most influential was the Carbonari. Founded in Naples around 1800 and modeled after an older French secret society, which itself borrowed most of its details from Freemasonry, the Carbonari (the name means "charcoal burners") had two degrees of initiation, apprentice and master. Members took their initiation oaths on the blade of an ax. Each initiate was required to have a rifle, fifty cartridges, and a dagger, and to be ready to use these at any moment in the cause of liberty and constitutional government.

The Carbonari first flexed their muscles in 1814, when revolts led by the order overthrew French-backed puppet governments throughout Italy. The years 1820 and 1821 saw Carbonari uprisings in Spain, Italy, and Greece; in 1830, a Carbonari-backed rising overthrew the French government; and in 1831, a Carbonari revolt shook Italy. Meanwhile the example set by the Carbonari inspired revolutionaries across Europe: the Decembrist rising in 1825 in Russia; the Fenian Brotherhood among Irish exiles in America from 1858 on; and many other revolutionary secret societies borrowed Carbonari ideas and practices for their own use.

Only in Greece, where the revolt of 1821 won the Greek people freedom after four centuries of Turkish rule, did the Carbonari succeed in their immediate goals; their other risings were defeated sooner or later by armed force. The threat of Carbonari risings, though, forced even the most diehard conservative nations to grant civil rights to their people. In this indirect way, the Carbonari achieved an impressive degree of success.

SEE ALSO: The Decembrists (1825), The Fenian Brotherhood (1858)

Episodio delle Cinque Giornate **(Episode of the five days),** a masterful c. 1885 painting by Baldassare Verazzi (1819–1886), depicts a five-day uprising in Milan, at the Palazzo Litta, March 18–22, 1848, in which the Carbonari were participants. The Carbonari were behind a series of uprisings—all in the cause of liberty and Italian unification.

THE SUBLIME PERFECT MASTERS

1809

THE DEFEAT OF THE CONSPIRACY OF Equals did nothing to cool the ardor of Filippo Buonarroti (1762–1837) for revolutionary conspiracy. When he was released from prison in 1806, he moved to Switzerland and immediately plunged back into political intrigues. He joined the Philadelphes, but that order's goal of overthrowing Napoleon was too tame for Buonarroti. In 1809, he founded a conspiracy of his own, the Sublime Perfect Masters, with the goal of overthrowing all governments of Europe and abolishing private property.

Recruits to the new order didn't learn its goals immediately. Members had to prove their loyalty to the order before being advanced through its ranks to the degree of Areopagite, where they learned of the existence of the secret coordinating body, the Grand Firmament. As the order expanded, Sublime Perfect Masters infiltrated many other liberal and radical organizations and helped coordinate their actions with the Grand Firmament's agenda.

The Sublime Perfect Masters largely directed the wave of uprisings that swept Europe in 1820 and 1821. Afterwards, though, secret police in several European countries managed to obtain details of the order's organization and efforts, launching a continent-wide panic. In 1828, as a result, Buonarroti changed the name of the order to The World. He also published a book, *Conspiracy for Equality*, about his experiences with the Conspiracy of Equals, which became the bible of liberal and radical secret societies until the early twentieth century. The World, however, did not long survive Buonarroti's death in 1837, and its members joined other radical conspiracies thereafter.

SEE ALSO: The Conspiracy of Equals (1796), The Philadelphes (1797)

The Italian-born French revolutionary Filippo Buonarroti, founder of the Sublime Perfect Masters, depicted in a nineteenth-century oil painting.

THE CHEVALIERS OF FAITH

NOT ALL THE SECRET SOCIETIES SET IN motion by the French Revolution were liberal or radical. There were also conservative conspiracies, and the most successful of them went by the innocuous label of the Chevaliers of Faith.

The founder of the order, Ferdinand de Bertier (1782–1864), was the son of a royal official murdered by the Paris mob during the Revolution. A royalist and a devout Catholic, Bertier became active in conspiracies against Napoleon, and went to jail in 1809. On his release the next year, he joined a Masonic lodge to learn how to run a secret society, and then founded the Chevaliers of Faith.

On paper, the order existed to carry out works of charity and Catholic piety. Members of the lower degrees learned no more than this. Only after advancing to the third degree, after careful vetting, did members discover that the order had a political agenda, and only the inner circle composed of members of the sixth degree learned that the heart of that agenda was the overthrow of Napoleon's regime.

By 1813 the Chevaliers of Faith had a substantial membership across much of France, and preparations for an insurrection began. In 1814, the order got its chance when Napoleon's armies suffered a series of disastrous defeats in Spain, and British and Spanish armies invaded the south of France. The Chevaliers went into action immediately, providing the invaders with detailed intelligence and guidance, and staging an uprising in Bordeaux that proclaimed Louis XVIII King of France. Napoleon's final defeat at Waterloo the next year marked the end of his regime, and also of the Chevaliers of Faith, which quietly faded away once its work was done.

SEE ALSO: The Conspiracy of Equals (1796), The Carbonari (1800)

The defeat of Napoleon's forces at Waterloo in June 1815, shown here in an unattributed painting of the battle at Hougoumont. For the Chevaliers of Faith, this was a long-sought victory. They faded away in the aftermath, but their primary objective—to see Napoleon unseated and his regime overthrown—had been accomplished.

THE DECEMBRISTS

ON THE MORNING OF DECEMBER 14, 1825, onlookers in St. Petersburg, the capital of the Russian Empire, were startled to watch three thousand heavily armed troops march into Senate Square and call on the rest of the Russian Army to rise in revolt. None of the other regiments in the capital responded to the call, and that afternoon, troops loyal to the tsar fired on the would-be revolutionaries, killing many and scattering the rest. Thus began and ended what, because of the date, writers then and now called the Decembrist revolt.

When the imperial government investigated, it discovered a web of conspiracy going back to the years immediately after the Napoleonic Wars. In 1816, an army officer named Pavel Pestel (1793–1826) founded the Union of Salvation, a secret society that aimed at abolishing serfdom and replacing the autocratic rule of the tsars with a constitutional monarchy. It fell apart the next year, but Pestel founded a new society, the Union of Welfare, in 1818. Over the years that followed, borrowing ideas from the Carbonari and the Bavarian Illuminati, the Union pursued a strategy of infiltration, recruiting members in the army and the civil service.

Like many conspiracies before and after, the members of the Union overestimated the success of their subversive methods, and their effort to seize power was a total failure. Over the long run, however, the Decembrist rising succeeded in convincing many Russians that reform was necessary—and the government's refusal to yield launched the spiral of revolt and repression that culminated in the Bolshevik coup d'état of 1917.

SEE ALSO: The Bavarian Illuminati (1776), The Carbonari (1800), The Russian Revolution (1917)

Au service des Tsars **(In the service of the tsars),** an 1853 painting by Vasily Timm (1820–1895), offers a dramatic view of three thousand troops, as they rode into Senate Square in St. Petersburg, Russia, on December 14, 1825. Their commanders, who were opposed to the new tsar, Nicholas I (1796–1855), hoped to rally support from the rest of the troops stationed in St. Petersburg, but their revolt was quickly and violently quashed by troops loyal to the tsar.

Assassinat de William Morgan, journaliste de New-York, qui, reniant la Franc-
Maçonnerie dont il avait fait partie, répara vaillamment sa faute en publiant, le premier,
les rituels de la secte (13 septembre 1826).

THE MORGAN AFFAIR

WILLIAM MORGAN (1774–1826), WAS not the kind of man that Freemasons in the United States usually admitted to their order in the 1820s, and there is some doubt that he ever was actually initiated into Masonry. A quarrelsome alcoholic constantly in trouble for unpaid debts, he somehow either got into a lodge or learned enough from published accounts of Masonic ritual to pass for a Mason. He certainly attended lodges in upstate New York in the early 1820s.

Then he quarreled with the Masons of Batavia, New York, quit the lodge there, and decided to revenge himself by publishing a book revealing the secrets of Freemasonry. While the book was in press, on September 12, 1826, witnesses saw Morgan struggling and shouting as four men forced him into a carriage. He was never seen again. To this day, no one is exactly sure what happened to him; one widely accepted theory was that he was held prisoner for several days at Fort Niagara, which had been abandoned after the War of 1812, and then was either murdered by his kidnappers and thrown into the Niagara River or drowned in the river while attempting to escape.

The kidnapping of William Morgan set off an explosion of anti-Masonic sentiment in the United States. The same fear of secret societies that had half of Europe quaking in its boots at the names of the Carbonari and the Bavarian Illuminati fastened onto Masonry in the United States. Over the years that followed, many American Masons quit their lodges and renounced Masonry, and Masonic membership dropped steeply and stayed low for decades thereafter. Not until after the Civil War did Freemasonry recover the status it had enjoyed at the time of the Revolutionary War.

SEE ALSO: The Bavarian Illuminati (1776), *Proofs of a Conspiracy* (1797), The Carbonari (1800), The Anti-Masonic Party (1828)

This engraving, by Pierre Méjanel, from Léo Taxil's *Mystères de la Franc-Maçonnerie*, (Mysteries of Freemasonry), published in Paris in 1866, illustrates the grisly fate of William Morgan. He fell afoul of the Masons of Batavia, New York, by publishing a book in 1826 revealing the secrets of Freemasonry. His body was never found.

Drawn from life and Engraved by J.B.Longacre.

WILLIAM WIRT.

THE ANTI-MASONIC PARTY

THE MORGAN AFFAIR, AS THE ABDUCTION and apparent murder of William Morgan came to be known, quickly took on a political dimension in the United States. In the wake of the scandal, public meetings in upstate New York denounced Freemasonry, demanded that known Masons be thrown out of public office, and called for new laws making Masonic oaths illegal. When the existing political parties showed no interest in this platform, the outraged citizens founded the first significant third party in American history, the Anti-Masonic Party.

The new party never succeeded in spreading beyond the Northeast, and it was only a significant power in five states—New York, Pennsylvania, Connecticut, Rhode Island, and Vermont. Its one attempt at the White House, in 1832, ran William Wirt (1772–1834) of Maryland and only carried the state of Vermont. During the ten years from its founding in 1828 to its dissolution in 1838, however, it elected one senator and twenty-four representatives to Congress, and became the majority party in several states, launching investigative committees in state legislatures and passing laws that penalized Masons and outlawed Masonic oaths.

The panic over Freemasonry generated by the Morgan Affair, though, faded as new crises racked the United States and new bogeymen caught the imaginations of the fearful. After the party's failed presidential run, most of its leaders joined the newly founded Whig Party, while many of its members were caught up in the rising tide of anti-Catholic agitation as immigration from Catholic countries became a political hot button and the Catholic Church replaced the Freemasons as America's bogeyman du jour.

SEE ALSO: The Morgan Affair (1826), The Know-Nothing Party (1849)

An engraving of William Wirt by James Barton Longacre (1794–1869), created c. 1810–1834. Wirt, a lawyer, statesman, and former Freemason, ran on the anti-Masonic ticket for president of the United States in 1832—and lost.

322

Thursday Evening, July 25, 1861.

☞ . VI   S. B. T.

Nisi in bonis amicitia esse non potest.

Cic. de Am. 5. 1.

C. L. Kitchel S. E. C.

YALE COLLEGE,
Thursday Evening, July 4. }

SKULL AND BONES

THE EARLY NINETEENTH CENTURY WAS THE seedtime of the American university fraternity. Inspired by German student societies and by fraternal orders such as Freemasonry, students across the growing United States created undergraduate associations that were part drinking club, part rooming house, and part secret society. By and large, conspiracy researchers have ignored the resulting fraternities and sororities; the one exception is Skull and Bones.

Founded at Yale University by fifteen undergraduates in 1832, Skull and Bones was originally called the Eulogian Society but changed its name the next year when it adopted the pirate flag as its emblem. As the most prestigious student society at one of America's top universities, Skull and Bones has had plenty of members who went on to become influential in politics and the business world, including three presidents—William Howard Taft (1857–1930), George H. W. Bush

(b. 1924), and George W. Bush (b. 1946)—and its members, influential and otherwise, look out for one another's interests, as of course do members of every fraternity and sorority.

Skull and Bones's reputation as one of America's most influential secret societies began in the early 1980s, as conspiracy beliefs originally created by the John Birch Society and other right-wing organizations found new adherents on the left. The disputed election of George W. Bush as U.S. president in 2000, however, helped launch a new wave of publicity surrounding Skull and Bones, as opponents of the Bush administration portrayed the fraternity as the sinister secret cabal behind the much-discussed new world order. All this colorful publicity must have thrilled the fraternity's undergraduate members.

SEE ALSO: *Trilateralism* (1980), The New World Order (1991)

An invitation for a Skull and Bones event, scheduled for July 25, 1861, with a quote from Cicero's *De amicitia*: "*Nisi in bonis amicitia esse non potest*" (No friendship can exist except in good men). Invitations from Skull and Bones sometimes included a pun on *bone*.

THE LEAGUE OF OUTLAWS

IN THE WAKE OF THE NAPOLEONIC WARS, ultraconservative governments ruled in most of Europe. Nowhere were their policies more resented than in Germany, which was still divided into a patchwork of little nations ruled by petty despots. Young Germans of radical political views thus very often ended up in exile in Paris. That was where Theodor Schuster (1808–1872) set out to found a revolutionary conspiracy among young German expatriates, the League of Outlaws.

Schuster modeled his organization on older revolutionary conspiracies such as the Raggi and the Sublime Perfect Masters, with local "tents" answering to provincial "camps" that took their orders from a central "focus." The goals of radical political conspiracy, though, had begun to shift as the spread of predatory industrial capitalism forced radicals to redirect their attention from politics to economics. Schuster's organization accordingly set out to abolish class differences, stop the exploitation of workers by capitalists, and establish a "cooperative republic" in which peasant cooperatives and government intervention would keep the capitalists in check.

Schuster's organizational skills were not up to the task of running a political secret society, however, and the League of Outlaws never attracted more than a few hundred members or came up with a viable plan for carrying out a revolution. A series of internal struggles beginning in 1836 crippled the organization, and it dissolved in 1838. By then, though, a new organization along the same lines—the League of the Just—had come on the scene, and through it Schuster's dream would be reshaped into the ideology of Communism.

SEE ALSO: The Raggi (1797), The Sublime Perfect Masters (1809), The League of the Just (1837), The First International (1864)

Revolutionaries in Berlin, Germany, in 1848, depicted by an unknown artist, c. 1848–1850. German radical groups found inspiration from Theodor Schuster, founder of the League of Outlaws, years after the organization dissolved in 1838.

THE LEAGUE OF THE JUST

A S THE LEAGUE OF OUTLAWS FELL APART in internal bickering, a group of its members in Paris set out to found a new organization that would build on its successes and avoid its failures. They named their new organization the League of the Just. Like its predecessor, it drew extensively on the experience of older revolutionary conspiracies such as the Carbonari and the Sublime Perfect Masters, but it redirected its attention toward the economic concerns of an era in which predatory industrial capitalism was heaping up fortunes for the few, while plunging the many into a new world of starvation wages and unsafe working conditions.

The League of the Just introduced democracy into its internal structure, allowing each of its local and regional units to elect their own leaders and make many of their own decisions. This had the unintended effect of turning the league into a debating society rather than an effective political conspiracy.

The league's headquarters had to relocate to London after civil unrest in 1839 in Paris led the French authorities to crack down on radical groups of all kinds. Allying with English radicals, the league found its feet again, but never did manage to do much toward the universal revolution for which its members longed.

In 1847, the leadership of the league encountered the writings of Karl Marx (1818–1883), then a journalist and radical theorist living in Brussels. Impressed by Marx's ideas, they changed their organization from a secret society to a political party, and took a new name—the Communist League. This did nothing to improve the league's effectiveness, and it went out of existence in the mid-1850s, but its last years helped to spread Marxist ideology through the European left.

SEE ALSO: The League of Outlaws (1834), The First International (1864)

The **Cologne communist trial in Germany in 1852** is depicted in this wood engraving made in 1852 by an unknown artist. Years earlier, the League of the Just, in thrall to the writing of Karl Marx, changed their orientation and name to the Communist League. The organization petered out in the 1850s, but Marxism continued to be challenged by courts such as the one pictured here.

THE COMMUNIST MANIFESTO

SPECTER IS HAUNTING EUROPE—THE specter of Communism." With these words, the opening lines of *The Communist Manifesto,* Karl Marx (1818–1883) and Friedrich Engels (1820–1895) launched the most successful of the political movements to come out of the golden age of conspiracies.

Marx and Engels did not invent the term *Communism*—it had been coined sometime in the 1830s, and first saw print in an 1840 newspaper article. Several French groups tried to lay claim to the label in the early 1840s, but Marx made it his own with a cascade of voluminous writings that proclaimed a revolution of the poor against the rich, after which private property would be abolished and farms and factories would be owned by the people who worked in them.

In the fetid industrial slums of nineteenth-century Europe, where the poor worked sixteen-hour days at starvation wages while the rich led lives of absurd extravagance, such ideas had a powerful appeal. The League of the Just, an influential German secret society, embraced Marx's ideas in 1847, changing its name to the Communist League; Marx and Engels wrote *The Communist Manifesto* to help promote the new organization.

Over the following years, Communism established itself as a radical ideology on the far left of the European political scene. The secret societies that dominated European radicalism after the Napoleonic Wars had accomplished few of their goals, and a new generation of radicals put their hopes in mass movements instead; thus Communist groups defined themselves as mass movements, even when the masses wanted nothing to do with them. Only after the first wave of Communist organizations failed utterly did Communists return to the old strategy of secrecy.

SEE ALSO: The League of the Just (1837), The First International (1864)

A portrait of Karl Marx, before 1875. Marx and Friedrich Engels wrote *The Communist Manifesto* to promote the Communist League, which had evolved from the League of the Just about twenty-five years earlier.

KNOW - NOTHINGISM IN BROOKLYN.

"None but citizens of the United States can be licensed to engage in any employment in this city."
Brooklyn Board of Aldermen.

THE KNOW-NOTHING PARTY

THE RISE OF IMMIGRATION FROM CATHOLIC countries to the United States became a hot-button issue in the early nineteenth century, and anti-Catholic secret societies promptly appeared in the new republic, paralleling the Orange Order in Ireland. The most influential of the newly founded secret societies, the Order of the Star-Spangled Banner, was founded in New York City in 1849 by Charles B. Allen. Its goals were to unite Protestants against the Catholic Church, keep Catholic politicians out of office, and lobby for a ban on immigration from Catholic countries. Members promised to answer any question about the order with the words "I know nothing," and this habit soon gave the order the nickname "the Know-Nothings."

In 1852, a political party with the same agenda, the American Party, was founded in New York City. Overlapping membership and identical goals soon led to a merger, and the united party absorbed several other anti-Catholic groups. At that time, the Federalist Party, one of the two oldest parties in U.S. politics, was in its death throes, and many former Federalists joined the Know-Nothings, giving the party a significant presence across the nation.

In 1854, a Know-Nothing candidate ran for governor of Maryland and won; the next year, a Know-Nothing governor took office in Tennessee. Encouraged, the Know-Nothings geared up for a run at the presidency in 1854. The order morphed into a political party, and nominated ex-president Millard Fillmore (1800–1874) as its candidate. In a three-way contest between Democrat James Buchanan (1791–1868) and John C. Fremont (1813–1890), the candidate of the recently founded Republican Party, the Know-Nothings came in third. Over the next few years, the slavery controversy took center stage in U.S. politics, and by the end of the Civil War the Know-Nothings were all but forgotten.

SEE ALSO: The Loyal Orange Order (1795)

A cartoon from *Frank Leslie's Illustrated Newspaper*, dated January 15, 1881. It perfectly expresses the "know-nothingism" made popular by the Order of the Star-Spangled Banner, a secret society for whom immigration from Catholic countries was anathema. Members of the society swore that they'd say, "I know nothing," if they were asked to divulge information about the organization.

AN AUTHENTIC EXPOSITION OF THE "K.G.C." KNIGHTS OF THE GOLDEN CIRCLE OR A HISTORY OF SECESSION

From 1834 to 1861.

By a MEMBER OF THE ORDER

ILLUSTRATED

ASHER & CO.
INDIANAPOLIS, IND.

THE KNIGHTS OF
THE GOLDEN CIRCLE

EORGE BICKLEY (1823–1867) WAS A MAN with a dream. A Southerner committed to the plantation system, he argued that the United States should carry out a campaign of conquest to the south, invading Mexico, Central America, and the Caribbean islands, settling them with white plantation owners and black slaves, and transforming them into American states. This "golden circle" of new slave states would also guarantee Southern domination of the United States. As a step toward his dream, he founded a secret society, the Knights of the Golden Circle, in 1854.

The Knights were quickly taken over by the Southern Rights Club, an organization of Southerners opposed to the abolition of slavery. As the Civil War approached, the Knights turned their efforts toward the project of Southern independence; and when the Civil War broke out in 1861, they repositioned themselves yet again to stir up dissension in Union territory.

In the Midwestern states, where a significant number of residents supported the Southern cause, the Knights of the Golden Circle soon became a significant force, interfering with Union enlistment drives, helping Confederate spies and prisoners of war escape back to the South, and smuggling contraband across the Confederate border. It also backed Clement Vallandigham (1820–1871), the leading antiwar politician in the Union, in his efforts to oppose Abraham Lincoln's war policies and support a peace treaty that would leave the Confederacy independent.

In 1863, Vallandigham ran for governor of Ohio and lost. In response, most members of the Knights of the Golden Circle turned to a more radical organization, the Order of American Knights, which abandoned the older order's political focus for a strategy of armed revolt.

SEE ALSO: The Order of American Knights (1863)

The book cover of *An Authentic Exposition of the Knights of the Golden Circle, A History of Secession from 1834 to 1861*, published in 1861 by an alleged member of the organization. The Knights of the Golden Circle presaged like-minded groups such as the Order of American Knights and the Ku Klux Klan.

THE CONSPIRACIES IN ST. PETERSBURG: THE NIHILISTS CARRIED TO EXECUTION.

THE NIHILISTS

THE RUSSIAN EMPIRE IN THE MIDDLE YEARS of the nineteenth century was a sprawling anachronism stuck halfway between the Middle Ages and the modern world. The tsar's court and the vast feudal estates of the nobility contrasted dramatically with the thriving universities and industrial concerns of Moscow and St. Petersburg. To young Russians longing for change, the coronation in 1855 of the young and liberal Tsar Alexander II (1818–1881), and a flurry of reforms that allowed Russians to travel and study abroad, seemed to mark the dawn of a hopeful new era.

The result was the birth of a counterculture, the New People, which prefigured nearly every detail of the hippie scene of the 1960s. Men grew their hair long, women bobbed theirs short and refused to wear makeup; unconventional clothing, blue-tinted spectacles, and chain-smoking cigarettes also featured in the New People's standard set of habits. Nikolai Chernyshevsky's 1863 novel *What Is To Be Done?*—the story of a young woman's journey from middle-class conformity to freedom among the New People—filled the same role for them that Jack Kerouac's novel *On The Road* did in the 1960s.

Like their hippie equivalents, the New People also got into radical politics, and the result was nihilism—a free blend of democratic ideals and terrorist ideology, generally carried out by small secret societies. As Alexander II's rule turned out to be less liberal than the New People had hoped, violence became the order of the day. In 1866, the tsar survived a nihilist assassination attempt; the crackdown on the New People that followed fed the nihilist movement. Further assassination attempts followed, and Alexander II finally was killed by a nihilist bomb in 1881. By then, a new generation of Russian radicals was taking inspiration from the writings of Karl Marx.

SEE ALSO: The Decembrists (1825), The Russian Revolution (1917)

This wood engraving, by an unattributed artist, shows Russian nihilists, tied to chairs on horse-drawn platforms, and being paraded past groups of soldiers on their way to execution in St. Petersburg, c. 1866.

From Erin's soil the Saxon foe
In shame shall be forever driven;
From Erin's sons who bear the woe,
The tyrants chain shall soon be riven,
And 'Erin's emerald isle shall be.
The Gem of Freedom in the sea.

FREEDOM TO IRELAND.

Then up and arm at Erin's call,
Ye FENIAN sons of Irish sires,
On every hill and mountain tall,
Arise and light your signal fires,
And swear to win with heart and hand,
The Freedom of your Native land.

THE FENIAN BROTHERHOOD

THE 1840S WERE A GRIM TIME IN IRELAND. A catastrophic potato blight and the indifference of the English colonial government had caused mass starvation and emigration—of the five million inhabitants of the Emerald Isle in 1840, two million died, two million fled the country, and only one million remained. An uprising against English rule in 1848 failed, and three of the leaders, John O'Mahony (1815–1877), Michael Doheny (1805–1863), and James Stephens (1825–1907), escaped to America. There, in 1858, they founded a secret society, the Fenian Brotherhood, to pursue Irish independence.

The Fenians posed a serious threat to British interests because of the huge Irish expatriate community in the United States, which numbered some 1.6 million in 1860. After the Civil War, thousands of veteran soldiers of Irish descent joined the order, giving it a core membership with nearly all the skills needed to carry out a revolution. Unfortunately for the Fenians, the one skill they lacked was the ability to keep a secret, and they soon became a public presence in Irish-American communities, holding regular meetings and annual conventions in the full glare of publicity. This made it easy for the English government to insert agents into the brotherhood and checkmate all its efforts.

As a result, every attempt the Fenians made to launch an insurrection was promptly betrayed to the English authorities and easily defeated. The most colorful of these attempts, an attempted invasion of Canada in 1866, was quickly dispersed by Canadian troops. An attempt to seize the English military arsenal at Chester Castle in England in 1867 failed just as completely. In the years that followed, the Brotherhood split into quarreling fragments, and the English became convinced—mistakenly—that they had nothing more to fear from the Fenians.

SEE ALSO: The Easter Rising (1916)

With severe poverty, starvation, a depressed economy, and widespread disgruntlement with British rule in Ireland, it was no wonder that secret groups like the Fenian Brotherhood, which was devoted to making Irish independence a reality, came into being in the United States—where almost half of Ireland had migrated, because of all the troubles at home. This Currier & Ives print, c. 1866, entitled *Freedom to Ireland*, expresses the bellicose spirit of groups like the Fenian Brotherhood.

REPORT

OF THE

JUDGE ADVOCATE GENERAL

ON

"The Order of American Knights,"

ALIAS

"THE SONS OF LIBERTY."

A Western Conspiracy

IN AID OF THE

SOUTHERN REBELLION.

———— ◆ ————

WASHINGTON, D. C.
CHRONICLE PRINT.
1864.

THE ORDER OF AMERICAN KNIGHTS

BY 1863, IT WAS CLEAR TO EVERYONE IN America that the Civil War would be fought out to the bitter end. Even though the Lincoln administration's draft laws were unpopular, young men across the North answered the call, providing the Union with an immense advantage in manpower. In response, many Confederate sympathizers in the Midwest were no longer willing to limit their efforts to the relatively peaceful methods pursued by the Knights of the Golden Circle, especially after that order's attempt to influence Union politics had failed.

The Order of American Knights was the logical result. Founded in St. Louis by Phineas C. Wright, it spread rapidly through the Midwest and attracted followers from as far east as New York State. It was organized on a military basis, with local companies in each county answering to a general in each state and a grand commander, the pro-Southern politician Clement Vallandigham, in exile in Canada. All through the second half of 1863 and the first half of 1864, the Knights gathered arms, trained recruits, and carried out guerrilla actions in the southern counties of Indiana and Illinois, waiting for the opportunity to rise up and break the Midwest away from the Union.

The planned uprising got under way in July 1864, but despite help from the Confederacy it was a dismal failure, easily crushed by Union troops. The order went out of existence shortly thereafter. Half a century after the Civil War, though, the same states where the Order of American Knights had flourished would become a major recruiting ground for the reborn Ku Klux Klan.

SEE ALSO: The Knights of the Golden Circle (1854), The Klan Reborn (1915)

Report of the Judge Advocate General on "The Order of American Knights," alias "The Sons of Liberty": A Western Conspiracy in aid of the Southern Rebellion, was published in 1864, by the United States Army, Office of the Judge Advocate, General Joseph Holt. This report, which is still in print, was the outgrowth of conspiracies, led by Confederate sympathizers, to break the Midwest away from the Union.

THE FIRST INTERNATIONAL

B Y THE 1850S THE PHILADELPHES, THE last of the great conspiracies to come out of the French Revolution, was a shadow of its former self. Exiled from France after the coup d'état that put Napoleon III in power, the Philadelphes regrouped in London. Their efforts to make common cause with other radical groups in Europe convinced them that a front group oriented toward the rights of working people might be an effective vehicle for their plans. In 1864, accordingly, Philadelphe members founded the International Workingmen's Organization—the International, for short— and began recruiting political radicals and trade-union members across Europe.

Among the many radicals who joined the new organization was a German economist named Karl Marx (1818–1883), also living in exile in London. Marx and his friend and patron Friedrich Engels (1820–1895) had become major figures in European radical circles with the 1848 publication of *The Communist Manifesto*, and the Philadelphes hoped that they could capitalize on Marx's fame for their own purposes. Marx proved to be better at political scheming than they were, though, and within a year of the organization's founding he was in charge of the International, and the Philadelphes had been expelled.

Marx had a major rival, though, in the Russian revolutionary Mikhail Bakunin (1814–1876), whose International Brothers quickly set out to infiltrate the International. A series of bruising political struggles left Marx still in control, but the struggle left the International fatally weakened. It went out of existence in 1876, and a new organization of the same kind—the Second International— did not take shape until 1889.

SEE ALSO: The Philadelphes (1797), *The Communist Manifesto* (1847), The International Brothers (1866), The Second International (1889)

An illustration of Mikhail Bakunin addressing members of the IWA (International Workingmen's Association), often called the First International, at the congress in Basle, Switzerland, in 1869. The rivalry between Bakunin and Karl Marx, a fellow radical and member of the "International," resulted in a weakened organization, but with Marx in control.

THE KU KLUX KLAN

PULASKI, TENNESSEE, IS A PLEASANT TOWN but not an exciting one, and after the Civil War it didn't offer much to keep young men busy. That may be why six Confederate veterans in that town decided to organize a secret society. They'd grown up reading stories about the Scottish clans, and one of them had enough education to know the Greek word *kuklos,* "circle"; at some point, the two got muddled together to create the name of their organization—the Ku Klux Klan.

The original Klansmen were simply interested in dressing up as ghosts and goblins to play pranks on their neighbors, but that light-hearted activity was soon replaced by something much uglier. New members joined and began using the same tactics to terrorize freed slaves and the Northern "carpetbaggers" who came South to try to remake Dixie in a Yankee image. By 1868, the Klan had thousands of members across the South and had recruited Confederate cavalry general Nathan Bedford Forrest (1821–1877) as its head. The original ghost costume was standardized into a white robe and pointed white hood with eyeholes, and Klansmen carried out a campaign of terror to keep newly enfranchised African Americans from exercising their civil rights.

Under the weak presidency of Andrew Johnson (1808–1875), the Klan faced few reprisals from the federal government. In 1869, though, Ulysses S. Grant (1822–1885) became president. Grant sent federal troops to the South and imposed martial law to break the back of the Klan. Thousands of actual and suspected Klansmen did time in federal prisons over the years that followed. By the late 1870s, the Klan was little more than a memory, and it would not be revived until 1915.

SEE ALSO: The Klan Reborn (1915), Anti-Klan Secret Societies (1923), The Klan Destroyed (1925)

A photo of General Nathan B. Forrest, considered one of the greatest Confederate cavalrymen of the American Civil War. In 1868, Forrest was recruited by the Klan to head the nascent organization, which had been founded three years earlier by six veterans of the Confederacy.

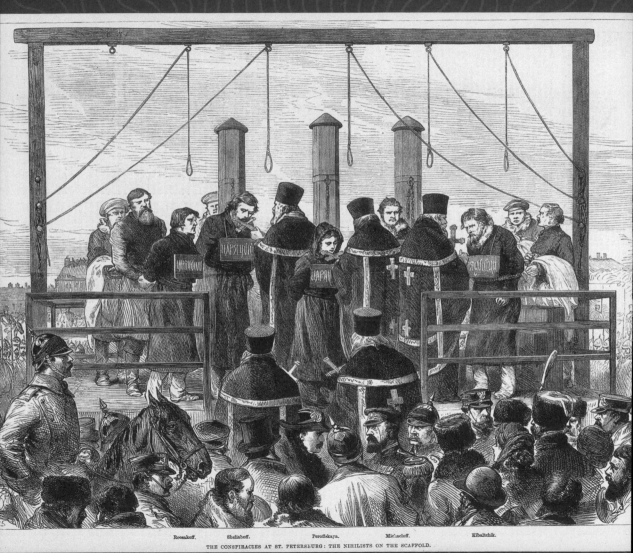

Rcssakoff.   Shcliaboff.   Peroffskaya.   Mic'.aeloff.   Kibaltchik.

THE CONSPIRACIES AT ST. PETERSBURG: THE NIHILISTS ON THE SCAFFOLD.

THE INTERNATIONAL BROTHERS

MIKHAIL BAKUNIN (1814–1876) WAS A veteran of the Russian nihilist movement and revolutionary underground. Like many Russian political radicals of the time, he ended up in exile and got involved in the broader world of European revolutionary politics. Sometime in the early 1860s, he began to put together an organization to further his political goals, calling it the International Brothers. In 1866, the publication of his manifesto, *A Revolutionary Catechism*, attracted attention and followers from the radical scene all over Europe.

The International Brothers, like some later groups, worked through systematic subversion. It started by organizing a front group, the Alliance of Social Revolutionists, which then formed another front group, the International Alliance of Socialist Democracy. In 1868, this merged with the First International, and Bakunin's followers proceeded to try to take over the First International and use it as yet another front group for their ambitions. Bakunin and his supporters had bitten off more than they could chew, though, because the First International had already been taken over by the followers of Karl Marx, and after four years of bitter struggle between Marxists and Bakuninists, Bakunin and his followers were forced out.

Bakunin then tried to launch a competing International, and failed. His cause was not helped by the discovery in 1874 that he had taken the entire treasury of the International Brothers and used it for home improvements on his Swiss villa. Once Bakunin died in 1876, the Brothers promptly dissolved; although the First International ceased to exist the same year, due to its own internal troubles, the way was clear for the founding of the Second International in 1889.

SEE ALSO: The First International (1864), The Second International (1889)

The first wave of Russian nihilism in the 1860s was followed by a second, more violent expression of the movement, which ended in 1881, with the assassination of Tsar Alexander II (1818–1881). In this wood engraving, c. 1881, five Russian nihilists are given Last Rites at the scaffold before their execution.

FIRST ANNUAL PICNIC OF THE "KNIGHTS OF LABOR"— MORE FUN FOR THE SPECTATORS THAN FOR THE PERFORMERS.

THE KNIGHTS OF LABOR

1869

A S THE NINETEENTH CENTURY PASSED ITS midpoint, the great wave of political conspiracy set in motion by the French Revolution began to morph in new directions. Economic justice became a theme as potent as democratic politics, and secret societies were pressed into service in that cause as well. That was what led to the rise of the Knights of Labor, a secret society that turned into America's first labor union.

The Knights of Labor was the brainchild of Uriah Stephens (1821–1882), a Philadelphia tailor and labor organizer who was active in Freemasonry and several other fraternal orders of the time. In 1869, when he founded the order, labor unions were illegal, and employers could fire anyone who was even suspected of belonging to one. The Knights thus used classic secret-society methods to keep their membership and meetings secret, and members took an oath never to reveal the names of other members on penalty of permanent expulsion.

Agitation against secret societies made these protective devices a political liability, though, and in 1882 the Knights of Labor transformed itself into a public labor union and opened its doors to women and African Americans. For the next few decades, the Knights of Labor were a significant force in American society and helped promote economic justice and workplace safety in the teeth of opposition from both political parties. As the nineteenth century drew to a close, though, the Knights' refusal to support sabotage and violence in labor disputes made it lose ground to newer and more radical unions such as the Industrial Workers of the World (IWW), the famous "Wobblies," and to Communist organizations affiliated with the Second International. The Knights went out of existence in 1917.

SEE ALSO: *The Communist Manifesto* (1847), The Second International (1889)

A cartoon from *Puck* magazine, c. 1882, by Joseph Ferdinand Keppler (1838-1894). It lampoons the challenging climb for working men and women to gain economic justice—that is, higher wages—or put more simply, enough money to buy bread! The Knights of Labor, pictured in the cartoon, were a secret society that morphed into America's first labor union, whose mission was to promote economic justice and safety in the workplace. In contrast, railroad tycoon Jason "Jay" Gould (1836-1892) and William Henry "Billy" Vanderbilt (1831-1895), then the richest man in America, are also shown, riding by in a carriage and taking in the scene with a bemused eye.

KNICKERBOCKER COTTAGE

Copyright 1909   S. Hollyer.

THE SHRINERS

THE ANCIENT ARABIC ORDER OF NOBLES OF the Mystic Shrine—the Shriners, for short—are perhaps the most unsecretive secret society in existence, a Masonic drinking club once widely known for their red fezzes, their wild conventions, their penchant for driving miniature cars in parades, and, on a more serious level, their creation and support of free hospitals and burn clinics for children. A less conspiratorial group is hard to imagine—but some conspiracy theorists have nonetheless identified the Shriners as the power behind the sinister new world order.

The order was founded in 1871 by Dr. Walter Fleming (1838–1913), a New York City physician, and a circle of Masonic friends who met for lunch at the Knickerbocker Cottage, a popular New York restaurant. At first nothing more than a drinking club for high-ranking Freemasons, it adopted an ornate initiation ritual in 1877 and took up charitable fundraising in 1888. Both these measures proved wildly popular and drove a dramatic expansion in the order's size and wealth.

During the first two thirds of the twentieth century, as the order reached its peak, the Shriners had facilities in every large city in the United States, equipped with golf courses and well-stocked bars, and national Shriner conventions became legendary as the wildest parties in the American fraternal scene. As Freemasonry has lost members and influence in the last decades of the twentieth century, in turn, Shriners have struggled to maintain the lavish habits of an earlier day, and creeping respectability has toned down the antics that once characterized Shriner events. Inevitably, these changes have failed to have any influence on the colorful claims about Shriners found in current conspiracy-theory literature.

SEE ALSO: The New World Order (1991)

1871

Knickerbocker Cottage, a restaurant in lower Manhattan where a group of Masons met in 1870, to discuss the founding of a new fraternity for Masons. One year later, with Dr. Walter Fleming at the helm, The Ancient Arabic Order of the Nobles of the Mystic Shrine, known today as Shriners International (or simply, the Shriners), was established.

A Typical Tent. The Occupants of This One Are Porter Garnett, George Sterling and Jack London.

THE BOHEMIAN GROVE

WHEN THE BOHEMIAN CLUB STARTED out in 1872, the gentlemen's club was a recognized social institution, providing meals, lodging, and congenial companionship for men in the middle and upper classes. In its early days, the Bohemian Club offered those benefits to San Francisco's burgeoning population of writers, artists, and intellectuals. As the club grew, however, it attracted members of the city's financial elite, and by the early twentieth century it was the most prestigious club in northern California.

In 1878 the club purchased a vacation property 65 miles north of San Francisco and began hosting a summer retreat there, with cabins, contests, and mock-serious ceremonies of the sort more often associated with teenage summer camps. The highlight of the retreat then, as now, is a ceremony in which an effigy of Dull Care is cremated by a flame from the Lamp of Fellowship, with the assistance of colorful fireworks. While the retreat was originally meant for members of the Bohemian Club, high-ranking political and economic figures began attending as guests. Today the annual Bohemian Grove retreat attracts many of the leading politicians, financiers, and corporate executives in America, with a guest list overlapping significantly with the Council on Foreign Relations and other organizations of the American elite.

Inevitably, so large a concentration of wealth and power has attracted attention from the conspiracy-minded. On the more gullible end of current conspiracy literature, the adolescent high jinks of the Cremation of Care have been transformed into a ritual of Satanic sacrifice, and the Bohemian Grove has been added to the already overloaded roster of conspiracies behind the new world order.

SEE ALSO: The Council on Foreign Relations (1921), The New World Order (1991)

A photograph of a tent at the Bohemian Grove, c. 1905, picturing its occupants, from left to right, literary luminaries Porter Garnett (1871–1951), George Sterling (1869–1926), and Jack London (1876–1916). The photo was published in *The Pacific Monthly,* by Porter Garnett in his story "Forest Festivals of Bohemia," in September 1907.

THE MAFIA COMES TO AMERICA

THE ISLAND OF SICILY HAS LONG BEEN ONE of the poorest regions of Italy, and in the late nineteenth century it offered few opportunities to those who wanted to improve their lives. On the far side of the Atlantic, by contrast, American farms and factories had an insatiable appetite for labor and offered wages that were princely by Sicilian standards. In response, in the late nineteenth and early twentieth centuries, more than a million Sicilians left their homes and immigrated to the United States. Among the traditions they brought with them was the Mafia, the traditional Sicilian organized-crime syndicate, which has existed on the island since the Middle Ages and remains a significant force there today.

Over the course of the 1880s, Mafia organizations thus began to establish themselves in the big port cities of America's Atlantic coast, running protection rackets, illegal lotteries, and prostitution in Italian American neighborhoods. They faced heavy competition at first from established organized-crime groups. Irish and Jewish immigrant gangs were already well established in these same cities. The Camorra, a criminal secret society from the Italian city of Naples, was also trying to establish itself in the United States at the same time as the Mafia. All these groups could be counted on to defend their turf against the Sicilian upstarts.

From 1880 to 1929, as a result, warfare between competing criminal gangs was the rule rather than the exception in urban America. Gun battles among competing gangs filled the newspapers, and the death toll among leading Mafiosi was high. It would take a new generation of gangsters with roots outside the traditions of Sicily to move past the rivalries of that era and launch the era of modern American organized crime.

SEE ALSO: Al Capone Becomes *Capo dei Capi* (1929)

A cartoon caricaturing the Mafia, published during the sensational trial of nineteen Italian men indicted for the murder of David Hennessy (1858–1890), New Orleans' Chief of Police, in 1890. The Mafia is depicted as a woman, masked and heavily armed (note "Mafia" emblazoned on her sash), as she attempts to intimidate jurors at the Hennessy trial.

THE ORDER OF THE WHITE ROSE

NOT EVERY SECRET SOCIETY FOUNDED IN the golden age of conspiracy was a significant threat to existing governments. The Order of the White Rose, founded by a coterie of British romantics and aristocrats in 1886, was one of the ones that wasn't. In a last feeble echo of the Jacobite secret societies of the previous century, its members hoped to depose Queen Victoria (1819–1901) from the British throne in favor of Princess Maria of Bavaria (1849–1919), the heir of the House of Stuart.

Behind the Order of the White Rose lay a widespread reaction against the grim industrial society Britain had become since the Industrial Revolution. Where other visionaries looked to a future in which the industrial system would be reshaped to fit human values, the members of the Order of the White Rose kept their eyes fixed firmly on the past. They condemned democracy and called for a restoration of the absolute rule of kings by divine right. Their name came from the white rose of York, the badge of the Jacobites during the risings of 1715 and 1745, but the order seems never to have tried the earnest political and military intrigues of those earlier rebels, and contented itself with romantic daydreams and a little timid propaganda.

Much of the difficulty the order faced was simply that, in late nineteenth-century Britain, romantic royalism attracted only a tiny following. The order managed to sponsor a museum exhibit on the Stuart kings of Britain in London in 1889, but newspapers that reported on the Order of the White Rose dismissed it as a sleepy little society more interested in ritual than in political action. Ignored by everyone, except its own members, the order lingered until the start of World War I and then went quietly out of existence.

SEE ALSO: The 'Fifteen (1715), The 'Forty-Five (1745)

Maria Theresa of Bavaria, shown here in a drawing based on an undated photo, attributed, simply, to Elviraz. Members of the Order of the White Rose plotted to overturn the British throne and replace Queen Victoria with the princess.

The National Committee for the Prevention of Destitution,

37, NORFOLK STREET, STRAND.

MRS. SIDNEY WEBB, D. Litt.

"We want to reach the heart of every man and woman of good will . . . . and induce them to enrol themselves in this new Crusade."

————o————

IT IS NOW POSSIBLE TO ABOLISH DESTITUTION.

THE FABIAN SOCIETY

RITAIN DURING THE VICTORIAN ERA WAS a difficult place to be a middle-class intellectual leftist. On the one hand, the most important political movements on the far left embraced the ideas of Karl Marx and denounced middle-class people as lackeys of the capitalist system; on the other, the Liberal Party was liberal in name only, and pursued a set of policies just as biased toward the rich as the Conservatives. The logical response was to start an organization for middle-class radicals, and the Fabian Society was duly founded by Thomas Davidson (1817–1885) in 1887.

The society took its name from the Roman general Fabius Maximus, who defeated the armies of Hannibal by avoiding pitched battles and using indirect tactics. This was also the Fabian Society's strategy. In place of the violent revolution of Marxist theory, the Society set out to make Britain a socialist nation by gradual reforms. Pressure on the Liberal and Conservative Parties did little, so the Fabian Society helped found and promote the Labour Party as a counterweight to existing political alliances.

The Fabian Society thus ranks as one of the more successful conspiracies of modern times. In the first half of the twentieth century, the Labour Party outflanked the once-mighty Liberal Party and reduced it to irrelevance, and then took power after World War II and instituted a great many socialist programs. While the inevitable conservative backlash eliminated some of these in the 1980s and 1990s, Britain today remains far more socialist than it was in 1887, and the resurgence of the Labour Party's socialist wing in recent British elections suggests that the Fabian Society's patient tactics may continue to pay off.

SEE ALSO: *The Communist Manifesto* (1847)

Martha Beatrice Webb, Baroness Passfield (1858–1943), labor historian, social scientist, and social reformer, was, with her husband Sidney James Webb, Baron Passfield (1859-1947), a driving force in socialist intellectual circles at the turn of the century, and a prominent member of the Fabian Society. Webb coined the term "collective bargaining" and helped found the London School of Economics.

PUCK.

THE AMERICAN POPE.

THE AMERICAN PROTECTIVE ASSOCIATION

IN THE LATE NINETEENTH CENTURY, ROMAN Catholic immigrants occupied roughly the same place in the conservative American imagination that Muslim immigrants have come to fill in more recent times. Many Americans feared that the Roman Catholic Church, which was still deeply involved in politics in Europe and Latin America, would leverage the United States' swelling Catholic population to exercise a similar role and erase the boundaries between church and state. Anti-Catholic politicians and pressure groups accordingly burgeoned. Inevitably there were also anti-Catholic secret societies, echoing the Know-Nothing Party of an earlier era, and the American Protective Association was the largest of these.

Founded in Clinton, Iowa, in 1887, it pursued a platform of lobbying against immigration, stripping Catholic religious property of tax-exempt status, and forcing public inspections of Catholic monasteries and nunneries, around which the mass media of the time had built up an impressive stock of colorful rumors. A decade after its founding, the American Protective Association had a membership between one and two million, and at least twenty members of Congress were known members.

Unlike other populist secret societies of the same era, the American Protective Association didn't mix its anti-Catholicism with racism. North of the Mason-Dixon Line, local Councils admitted black men to full membership, while in the Southern states the Association maintained separate black and white Councils. It remained a significant presence in American political life until after World War I, when the reborn Ku Klux Klan added the Catholic Church to its long list of enemies.

SEE ALSO: The Know-Nothing Party (1849), The Klan Reborn (1915), The American Protective League (1917)

An anti-Catholic cartoon by Udo J. Keppler (1872–1956), published in *Puck* magazine in 1894, shows Cardinal Francesco Satolli (1839–1910), who was appointed in 1893 as the first Papal Delegate to the United States, casting an evil shadow across the country. The cartoon expresses the anti-immigration policy espoused by organizations such as the American Protective Association, particularly their paranoia about the supposed power of the Roman Catholic Church to erode the boundaries of church and state in the United States.

MAY-DAY-PARADE-N.Y.

May Day Parade. N.Y.

THE SECOND INTERNATIONAL

THE COLLAPSE OF THE FIRST International in 1872 did not mean the end of the radical Marxist ideology it favored, though many conservatives at the time hoped this was the case. In most of the nations of Europe, union organizers and radical parties became steadily more influential among the working classes as the human toll of the Industrial Revolution grew more extreme. In 1889, representatives from an assortment of trade unions and socialist parties in Britain, France, and Germany met in Paris to organize a new International.

Though it held annual conferences and hammered out a common platform dedicated to defending the interests of working people, the Second International was little more than a debating platform. Real power remained with the trade-union confederations and socialist parties in each nation. Despite the resulting weakness, the International succeeded in making socialism a recognized political and economic option in Europe, and helped build successful socialist parties in many European nations.

The most important project of the Second International, however, was a scheme to keep war from happening again in Europe. As the strains that would lead to World War I grew, the socialist parties that belonged to the International drew up a plan to launch simultaneous general strikes in every nation that declared war. When war broke out in 1914, however, not one socialist party followed through on the plan. Patriotism trumped socialism, the socialist parties fell into line behind the governments, and the Second International promptly imploded, leaving the field clear for the Third International of the postwar era.

SEE ALSO: *The Communist Manifesto* (1847), The First International (1864), The Third International (1919)

A photo of a May Day parade in New York City c. 1900, also known as International Worker's Day and Labour Day or Workers' Day in some countries. In 1904, the Sixth Conference of the Second International called on all Social Democratic party organizations and trade unions of all countries to demonstrate on May 1 for the legalization of the eight-hour workday, among other demands.

Der Bolschewismus von Moses bis Lenin

Zwiegespräch
zwischen

Adolf Hitler
und mir

Von

Dietrich Eckart †

Hoheneichen-Verlag München, Hildegardstraße 9

Hermann Göring

Die Geheimnisse der Weisen von Zion

„Alles dieses wußte ich schon vor 11 Jahren; wie ging es aber zu
daß ich es doch nicht glauben wollte?"

Ludwig XVI. bei seiner Verhaftung am 22. Juni 1791 in Varennes.
Vergl. Joh. Scherrs „Ueber Geheime Gesellschaften und deren Ge-
fährlichkeit für Staat und Religion", deutsche Uebersetzung nach der
5. englischen Auflage, Königsbrück bei W. Calenmann 1900, 142. Seite.

herausgegeben
im Auftrage des Verbandes gegen
Überhebung des Judentums E. V.

von

Gottfried zur Beek

7. Auflage

Verlag „Auf Vorposten" in Charlottenburg 4
1922

THE PROTOCOLS OF THE
ELDERS OF ZION

ONE OF HISTORY'S MOST EFFECTIVE works of disinformation, *The Protocols of the Elders of Zion* was created around 1895 by Yuliana Glinka (1844–1918), a Russian noblewoman working for the Tsarist secret police, and originally circulated by conservative and anti-Semitic circles in Russia and abroad. It purports to be the secret plan for world conquest adopted by a secret meeting of Jewish leaders—the "Elders of Zion"—at some unspecified place and time, setting out a vast campaign of subversion and financial manipulation intended to bring Christian Europe to its knees and establish a worldwide Jewish empire.

The text of the *Protocols* is almost entirely plagiarized from earlier writings, ranging from a French satire on the politics of Napoleon III to a vast range of nineteenth-century anti-Semitic literature. Despite these borrowings, many of which were pointed out early in its history, the *Protocols* were enthusiastically embraced by Russian anti-Semites before the Russian Revolution. Refugees from the new Communist regime thereafter brought it with them to Germany and other Western nations, where it was promptly translated and published.

The rising Nazi Party in Germany made it central to their propaganda, and after Hitler took power in 1933, it became required reading in German public schools. When the collapse of the Nazi regime and the revelation of its appalling human-rights abuses made anti-Semitism temporarily unfashionable in the Western world, in turn, the *Protocols* were promptly repurposed by other conspiracy theorists for their own uses. It remains in print today, and its claims have been repeatedly repurposed by other groups, under other names, such as the John Birch Society.

SEE ALSO: The Black Hundreds (1905), The German Workers Party (1919), Hitler Takes Power (1933), The John Birch Society (1959)

This 89-page pamphlet by Dietrich Eckart (1868–1923), *Bolshevism from Moses to Lenin: A Dialogue between Adolf Hitler and Me*, was published posthumously in 1925 and is still in print today. The dialogue is based on the authors' perception of civilization as a clash between Aryan and Jewish worldviews. Anti-Semites in Germany, such as Eckart and Hitler, were influenced by *The Protocols of the Elders of Zion*, purportedly a plot by Jewish leaders to override Christian Europe and establish their own hegemony. It was the centerpiece of the Nazi's anti-Semitic propaganda. Eckart, Hitler's mentor, was one of the founders of the Deutsche Arbeiterpartei, which morphed into the Nazi Party.

CHEZ TOUS LES LIBRAIRES ET Mds. DE JOURNAUX
LES MYSTÈRES
DE LA
FRANC-MAÇONNERIE
DÉVOILÉS
PAR
LÉO TAXIL
A LA GLOIRE DU GRAND
ARCHITECTE DE L'UNIVERS
MENDÈS
BAPHOMET
ANCIEN MEMBRE
DE LA RESP∴ LOGE
LE TEMPLE
DES AMIS DE L'HONNEUR FRANÇAIS
DU GRAND ORIENT DE FRANCE
La 1ère Livraison est GRATUITE
CHAQUE LIVRAISON SUIVANTE
SE VEND 10 CENTIMES
DEUX LIVRAISONS CHAQUE SEMAINE — UNE SÉRIE TOUS LES QUINZE JOURS
LETOUZEY ET ANÉ, ÉDITEURS, 17, Rue du Vieux Colombier, PARIS

THE "PALLADIAN ORDER" HOAX

WELL BEFORE THE DOORS OF THE HALL opened, a crowd waited on the street outside. Tickets had sold out weeks before. Lurid posters all over Paris explained why: Diana Vaughan, the former Grand Priestess of the sinister Palladian Order, was about to tell all.

The Palladian Order had been in the news since 1884, when a journalist named Léo Taxil (1854–1907) suddenly renounced his Masonic membership and returned to the Catholic Church. In a series of sensational books and articles thereafter, Taxil explained that he had left Masonry after discovering that it was controlled from within by a secret society of Satanist sex fiends, the Palladian Order. All this was music to the ears of conservative Catholics, and Taxil was lionized in the Catholic press and received a private audience with the pope in 1887. Each year brought revelations more titillating than the last, culminating with Diana Vaughan's lurid career as Grand Priestess, followed by her repentance and conversion to Catholicism.

By 1897, both the media and the Catholic hierarchy were beginning to ask Taxil the questions they should have asked from the beginning, and Taxil duly rented a hall for Vaughan to speak. When the hour came, though, it was Taxil who appeared on stage. He calmly informed the audience that "Diana Vaughan" was his typist, and had done none of the things he had claimed for her. For thirteen years he had made fools of them all, manufacturing absurd stories about the Freemasons to make fun of the Catholic Church. He then left the stage, just in time to escape the riot that followed. Ironically, a hundred years after this revelation, some of Taxil's fabrications were still being retailed by fundamentalist critics of Freemasonry.

SEE ALSO: *In Eminente* (1738)

A poster, printed in France in 1896, advertising Léo Taxil's sensational anti-Freemasonry book, available as a serial in bookstores and at magazine stands. Note that the imagery in the poster is based on Eliphas Lévi's version of Baphomet (an icon commonly associated with a goat-headed diabolical idol allegedly worshiped by the Knights Templar during the thirteenth and fourteenth centuries), rather than a Masonic image.

THE BLACK HUNDREDS

IN 1905, THE SPRAWLING RUSSIAN EMPIRE was in turmoil. In theory, Russia was one of the world's great powers; in practice, it had just suffered a humiliating defeat in the Russo-Japanese war of 1904–1905, its economy had been whipsawed by repeated crises, and its ruler, Tsar Nicholas II (1868–1918), was weak and incompetent. In an attempt to head off revolution, the tsar's ministers bullied him into granting limited civil rights and calling Russia's first Parliament, the Imperial Duma. Nicholas himself and a cadre of aristocrats wanted nothing more than to return to the good old days of imperial autocracy, but political concerns made it impossible for them to act openly.

That was when V. M. Purishkevich (1870–1920), a conservative activist, came into the picture. In 1905 he founded an organization called the Union of the Russian People, with the goal of convincing the masses that civil rights and democratic institutions were all part of the evil Jewish plot detailed in the forged *Protocols of the Elders of Zion*. The Black Hundreds, as the organization came to be called, pursued the same two-pronged strategy as other reactionary secret societies: overtly, it ran candidates for office and backed laws limiting civil rights; covertly, it organized armed bands to carry out a campaign of violence against political opponents and ethnic and religious minorities.

The Black Hundreds received substantial funding from the Russian government, and the Russian police and court system ignored its violent activities. Far from propping up the imperial system, though, the activities of the Black Hundreds simply fed the rising spiral of revolutionary violence that brought down the Tsarist regime in 1917.

SEE ALSO: *The Protocols of the Elders of Zion* (1895), The Russian Revolution (1917)

In this photo, strikers carrying flags and portraits of Tsar Nicholas II parade through the streets of Odessa during the Russian Revolution of 1905, an uprising that was instrumental in forcing the tsar to abandon autocratic rule and replace it with a constitutional monarchy.

-----Theozoology------

or the Science of the Sodomite Apelings and
the Divine Electron. An introduction to the
most ancient and most modern philosophy
and a justification of the monarchy and the
nobility. With 45 Illustrations.

THE ORDER OF NEW TEMPLARS

SOME CONSPIRACIES HAVE IDEOLOGIES that make sense—and then there was the Order of New Templars. This odd secret society was the brainchild of Austrian occultist Jörg Lanz von Liebenfels (1874–1954), a defrocked Catholic monk who became convinced that the original Aryans were blond, blue-eyed gods from another world, who had strange electropsychic powers, but had become addicted to deviant sex with subhuman ape-things and so produced modern humanity. Only those humans with enough of the primordial Aryan ancestry, he argued, could regain the lost electropsychic powers of the Aryan gods, and he claimed to be able to teach sufficiently pure Aryans how to do it.

Lanz's magnum opus, *Theozoology, or the Lore of the Sodom-Apelings and the Electron of the Gods*, was published in 1905 and made an immediate hit on the more credulous end of the central European right-wing occult scene.

The Order of New Templars established its headquarters in a castle in Austria donated by a wealthy supporter. The order published a magazine, *Ostara*, that combined articles on occultism and Lanz's teachings on theozoology with racist and anti-Semitic rants, calling for the exclusion of Jews and foreigners from an Aryan homeland.

The magazine had plenty of subscribers, but one in particular would become famous later—a young artist living a hand-to-mouth existence in Vienna in the years before World War I, who scraped together the money to pay for a subscription and buy the back issues of *Ostara*. Many of the ideas he took from Lanz's magazine would end up being put into practice in Germany after the war. The young artist's name, of course, was Adolf Hitler.

SEE ALSO: Fall of the Knights Templar (1307), Ariosophy (1908), The German Workers Party (1919)

The front cover of Jorg Lanz von Liebenfels' bizarre book, *Theozoology—or the Science of the Sodomite Apelings and the Divine Electron* (published in 1905), perhaps one of the strangest books ever published. (It is still in print.) The Order of New Templars embraced Lanz's book nevertheless and published the author's teachings on theozoology, filtered through a racist and anti-Semitic lens, in their magazine, *Ostara*.

ARIOSOPHY

B Y THE FIRST YEARS OF THE TWENTIETH century, the Austro-Hungarian Empire was a creaking anachronism, with the German-speaking upper class clinging to the customs of an earlier day in an attempt to keep their privileged position against a mostly Slavic underclass. Dreams of ancient German heroes and legends were hot properties in the popular culture of the time, and it was inevitable that someone would eventually use those as the basis for a secret society.

Guido von List (1848–1919), a popular Austrian author, proceeded to fill that niche. His books claimed to reveal the secret lore of the Armanen, a caste of ancient Germanic wizard-priests. That claim attracted a huge following, and in 1908 his fans founded the Guido von List Society to spread his teachings. In contrast to Theosophy, with its gospel of racial equality, List's followers came to call his teachings *Ariosophy*, "the wisdom of the Aryans." At some point after the society was founded, a secret inner circle—the Höhere Armanen-Orden (Higher Armanen Order)—was organized to further the Ariosophical cause by the usual secret society methods.

In his last years, as World War I shattered Europe's old order and sent the Austro-Hungarian Empire to its grave, von List began to speak of the coming of "the Strong One from Above," a heroic leader who would restore the Armanen mysteries and return the Germanic peoples to their supposed rightful place as rulers of the world. He died in 1919, just as a young Austrian military veteran named Adolf Hitler set out to fulfill that prophecy.

SEE ALSO: The Order of New Templars (1907), The Germanenorden (1912), The Thule Society (1918), The German Workers Party (1919), Hitler Takes Power (1933)

Guido von List, in a photo taken by Conrad Hubert Schiffer in 1909. Von List was a proponent of Ariosphy, loosely defined as "the wisdom of the Aryans." Von List's writings are thought to have prefigured the ascendancy of Adolf Hitler.

Rudolf von Sebottendorff

Bevor Hitler kam

Urkundliches aus der Frühzeit der nationalsozialistischen Bewegung

THE GERMANENORDEN

THE ARIOSOPHY OF GUIDO VON LIST FOUND a ready audience in Germany, and Ariosophical secret societies promptly took shape. The most influential of these was the *Germanenorden*, or Order of Germans. Hermann Pohl, its founder, was a member of the Reichshammerbund, the most active anti-Semitic organization in Germany before World War I. He believed devoutly in the existence of a vast Jewish conspiracy and decided that the only way to fight it was to organize an opposing conspiracy. The Germanenorden was the result.

In 1911, Pohl drafted a set of rituals for the order, and formed the first lodge of the new order, the Wotan Lodge, to test and revise the rituals and organizational structure. The next year, the Germanenorden was formally founded and began recruiting members by way of the Reichshammerbund. The order spread rapidly; within a year of its founding, it had six lodges and over five hundred members, and continued to expand thereafter, becoming a major presence in right-wing German nationalist circles.

Serious disagreements soon plagued the Germanenorden, though, with one faction seeking to pursue the order's goals through ritual and occult means, and another urging political conspiracy and assassination as more direct means. In 1916, as a result of these conflicts, the order split in two. Ironically, it was the order founded by the occultists, the Germanenorden Walvater, that ended up being drawn most deeply into politics as World War I ended, as its Munich lodge—by that time renamed the Thule Society—set off the chain of events that led to the birth of the Nazi Party.

SEE ALSO: The Order of New Templars (1907), Ariosophy (1908), The Thule Society (1918), The German Workers Party (1919), The SS (1925), Hitler Takes Power (1933)

The cover of *Bevor Hitler kam* (Before Hitler came), published in 1933. The author, Rudolf von Sebottendorff (1874–c. 1945), was a Freemason, occultist, and political activist who became involved with the Germanenorden around 1916. Not long after, he took on an important role in the Thule Society, an organization that would regroup under various names; one of them was the German Workers' Party, which, by 1920, would be reorganized by Adolf Hitler into the National Socialist German Workers' Party— that is, the Nazi Party.

THE KLAN REBORN

Bᴺ 1915 ᴛʜᴇ Kᴜ Kʟᴜx Kʟᴀɴ ᴡᴀꜱ ʟɪᴛᴛʟᴇ more than a memory, even in the most segregated corners of the American South; but a new technology would change that. One of the first full-length motion pictures, *The Birth of a Nation*, by D. W. Griffith (1875–1948), premiered that year and became the newborn movie industry's first major financial success.

The film is a portrayal of the Ku Klux Klan as heroic defenders of Southern values spawned a flood of imitators. The most successful of these was William J. Simmons (1880–1945), an enthusiastic promoter of secret societies, who founded The Knights of the Ku Klux Klan in 1915, with himself as Imperial Wizard. He wrote new rituals notable for an obsession with the letters *kl*; a lodge of the Klan was a *Klavern*, its meetings were *Klonvocations*, its officers included the *Klaliff*, the *Kligrapp*, and the *Kludd*. Inevitably, the book of rituals for the new Klan was titled the *Kloran*. Simmons had the good sense to hire a professional marketing firm to promote the new organization, and it grew rapidly after World War I. It counted 100,000 members by 1921 and more than four million by 1924.

Central to the new Klan's success was a broadening of the original Klan's focus on racial issues. Under Simmons's leadership, Roman Catholics, Jews, immigrants, trade unionists, and liberals joined African Americans on the Klan's hate list. Publicly, the Klan limited its actions to protest marches, boycotts, and voter-registration drives. On a more covert level, violence and intimidation played a central role in Klan strategy, publicly rejected by the national leadership but carried out systematically by local Klansmen under the protection of their hooded robes.

SEE ALSO: The Ku Klux Klan (1865), Anti-Klan Secret Societies (1923), The Klan Destroyed (1925), The Cagoule (1935)

D. W. Griffith's motion picture *The Birth of a Nation* was one of the movie industry's first blockbusters when it was released in 1915. The film, which glorified the Ku Klux Klan as saviors of the South during Reconstruction, revived interest in the organization. In fact, the Klan used the film—considered by many to be nothing less than racist propaganda, albeit extremely effective propaganda—to recruit new members for their organization.

THE EASTER RISING

B Y 1916 THE BRITISH GOVERNMENT WAS considering the Fenian Brotherhood a spent force. There were still Fenian groups active in Dublin and elsewhere, and terrorist acts against British rule over Ireland took place from time to time, but British officials believed they had nothing to fear from an old-fashioned secret society that had failed so many times before.

What no one in London realized was that a new generation of leaders had taken over the brotherhood, learned the lessons of past failures, and turned it into a small, efficient, and tautly disciplined revolutionary secret society. Rather than trying to organize a mass movement on their own, Fenian members concentrated on making connections to existing Irish militia groups and pro-independence political parties.

The coming of World War I convinced the Fenians that the time for rebellion had arrived. As British armies floundered and died in the bloody stalemate of the Western Front, the Fenian Brotherhood smuggled in arms and ammunition and prepared to act. On Easter weekend, 1916, the rising began, achieving total surprise and seizing several important targets in Dublin.

British officials scrambled to respond, and after several days of heavy fighting, the rising was defeated. The weakness of the British grip on Ireland, however, was impossible to miss. In the wake of the Easter Rising, a guerrilla war against the British began. By 1921 the British had had enough, and, for the first time since the reign of Queen Elizabeth I (1533–1603), Ireland was once again an independent nation. As events in Russia the next year would prove, the era of the revolutionary secret society was far from over.

SEE ALSO: The Fenian Brotherhood (1858), The Russian Revolution (1917)

Irish Citizen Army (ICA) soldiers firing from rooftops in Dublin during the Easter Rising of 1916. The ICA was a small, but well-trained paramilitary group of volunteers established in Dublin for the purposes of protecting workers' demonstrations from the police. Their comrades in arms, the Fenian Brotherhood, were the predecessors of the IRA (Irish Republican Army).

TAKE UP THE SWORD OF JUSTICE

THE AMERICAN PROTECTIVE LEAGUE

THE GOLDEN AGE OF CONSPIRACIES spawned vast numbers of secret societies that aimed at *overthrowing* governments, but very few that set out to *protect* one. Among the exceptions was the American Protective League, organized by the U.S. government in 1917.

By 1917, war had been raging in Europe for three long years. The Western Front was frozen in stalemate, while the Eastern Front was in chaos as Russia plunged into revolution. The United States had been bankrolling the Allies since early in the war, but money was no longer enough. The sinking of the *Lusitania* by a German submarine and a series of German diplomatic blunders provided an excuse for intervention, and Congress duly declared war.

Among the risks American officials feared, the threats of spying and sabotage were high. America was full of immigrants from Germany and the Austro-Hungarian Empire, the leading nations on the other side of the war, and no one knew for sure how many secret agents might have been planted in immigrant communities in advance of American intervention. The Bureau of Investigation (BOI), the former name of the FBI, in charge of counterintelligence, had too few agents to guard every potential target.

The American Protective League was the logical answer. The league was organized like any other secret society, but its members were enrolled as unpaid secret agents for the duration of the war. Each member reported suspicious activities to the head of the local lodge, who forwarded reports to the nearest BOI office. By the end of the war, the league had more than 250,000 members. It may not be accidental that the tactics it used were adopted by several of the anti-Klan secret societies in the postwar years.

SEE ALSO: Anti-Klan Secret Societies (1923)

British propaganda posters like this one (1920), showing the sinking of the *Lusitania* by the Germans in 1915—and which cries "Take up the Sword of Justice"—helped plead the case for the United States' intervention in World War I.

THE RUSSIAN REVOLUTION

B Y 1917, THE RUSSIAN EMPIRE WAS A basket case. Like France in 1789, it was an antique feudal monarchy pretending to be a modern nation-state, riddled with graft and incompetence, which ruled by fear rather than loyalty. All that was needed was a crisis, and when Russia was among the first countries to begin the mobilization that ended up starting World War I in 1914 and then suffered the first of a series of humiliating defeats from the smaller but far more competent German Army, the crisis had arrived.

The war cut Russia off from its overseas markets and plunged the Russian economy into chaos. As the government of Tsar Nicholas II (1868–1918) floundered and one military defeat followed another, popular unrest reached the boiling point. On February 22, 1917, workers at a munitions plant in St. Petersburg went on strike against the government, rioting broke out, and troops sent to quell the rioters joined them instead. On March 2, Nicholas II was forced to abdicate. The provisional government that took his place tried to avoid peace with Germany or fundamental reforms at home, and soon lost what little popular support it had. In October, the Bolsheviks, a radical Communist faction headed by Vladimir Lenin (1870–1924), staged a successful coup d'état against the provisional government and founded the Soviet Union.

The success of the coup, and the victory of the Communist forces in the civil war that followed, was an immense shock to people around the world. In 1917, most people dismissed Communism as an ideology of the lunatic fringe with no chance of taking power. As the Soviet regime cemented its power, many people who had dismissed conspiracy theories out of hand began to reconsider them.

SEE ALSO: The Decembrists (1825), *The Communist Manifesto* (1847), The Nihilists (1855), The Second International (1889), The John Birch Society (1959)

Vladimir Lenin at the Second All-Russian Congress of Soviets of Workers' and Soldiers' Deputies, held in Smolny in Petrograd on October 25-27, 1917, in a contemporary painting. The All-Russian Central Executive Committee and Council of People's Commissars named Lenin the chairman, making him the leader of the world's first Communist state.

THE THULE SOCIETY

IN 1917, RUDOLF VON SEBOTTENDORFF (1875–1945), a German-Turkish adventurer and occultist, joined the Germanenorden Walvater, the more occult-oriented of the two surviving fragments of the original Germanenorden. An effective organizer, von Sebottendorff quickly launched a lodge of the order in Munich, where he lived, and attracted more than 1,500 members, including Bavarian aristocrats and military officers. To deflect suspicions, the Munich lodge carried out its activities under the cover name of the Thule Society, and claimed to be a private organization for the study of ancient Germanic folklore. Its emblem was the swastika—a symbol that would shortly become much more famous.

When Germany lost World War I and the imperial government collapsed, a socialist government seized power in Munich and was quickly supplanted by a hard-line Communist faction. Munich descended into open warfare as conservatives, fearing a repeat of the Russian Revolution, rose against the new regime. The Thule Society played a central role in coordinating the counterrevolution, and raised a militia of its own that fought in the battles that ended the Bavarian Socialist Republic in May 1919.

To try to attract members of the working class away from Marxism, Sebottendorff talked two Thule members into launching a Workers Circle. In 1919 the circle morphed into a political party, the German Workers Party, but failed to get much done until September of that year, when an army veteran named Adolf Hitler came to visit one of its meetings.

SEE ALSO: Ariosophy (1908), The Germanenorden (1912), The German Workers Party (1919), The SS (1925), Hitler Takes Power (1933)

A bust of Rudolf von Sebottendorff, c. 1933, by Bavarian sculptor Hans Goebl (1901–1986), who produced several works of art for the Nazis during the 1930s and 1940s. Sebottendorff, a German occultist, founded the Thule Society in August 1918, as the Munich branch of the Germanenorden, a secret society, also known as the "Order of Teutons."

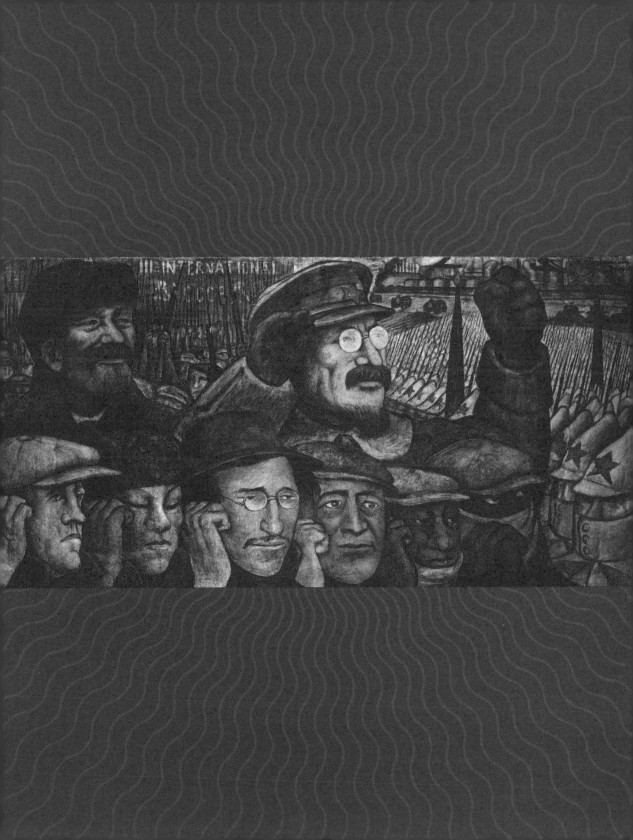

THE THIRD INTERNATIONAL

THE VICTORY OF VLADIMIR LENIN'S Bolshevik Party in the Russian Revolution, and the civil war that followed it, sent shockwaves through leftist political parties around the world. After so many failures, not least the embarrassing collapse of the Second International's plan to stop World War I, the fact that a party of the far left had taken over the world's largest nation gave new hope to radicals everywhere. Those hopes were cemented when a third International, the Communist International (Comintern for short), was founded in Moscow in 1919.

The rejoicing proved to be misplaced. To Lenin, and even more to his successor Joseph Stalin (1878–1953), the Comintern was simply an instrument of Soviet foreign policy, and political parties that joined it were expected to obey orders from Moscow without question, even when those orders violated the official policies of the Comintern. As a result, in the years following 1919 leftists in most European and many other countries split into two warring camps, one aligned with the Comintern and one opposed to it. The subservience of Comintern-affiliated parties to Moscow also played into the hands of radicals on the other side of the political spectrum, who used the many atrocities committed by the Soviet Union as propaganda against local leftist parties.

As an instrument of Soviet policy, the Comintern was a success and assisted Stalin's regime in placing spies all through the Western world. In terms of the old struggle to better the lot of the working classes, though, it was a complete disaster. By the time it was dissolved in 1943, many people around the world dismissed socialist parties as Soviet front groups—a habit that assisted the rise of later anti-Communist groups such as the John Birch Society.

SEE ALSO: The First International (1864), The Second International (1889), The John Birch Society (1959)

This 1933 mural by Diego Rivera (1886–1957), which now hangs in the Museo del Palacio de Bellas Artes in Mexico City, captures the spirit of The Third International—the Communist International (better known as the Comintern)—in March 1919. Lenin is very much in his element here.

Deutsche Volkspartei

Durch Arbeit zu Brot

Wählt Liste Moldenhauer

M. DUMONT SCHAUBERG, KÖLN.

THE GERMAN WORKERS PARTY

ORPORAL ADOLF HITLER (1889–1945) was not impressed. The young Austrian veteran had been hired by the German army to look into radical political organizations in Munich, and on the evening of September 12, 1919, his job took him to a meeting of the little German Workers Party. He noted in his memoirs that the party was so disorganized it didn't even have a rubber stamp to put a return address on envelopes. In the course of the evening's meeting, though, he got into a heated discussion with one of the other people present, and the members of the party were so moved by his passionate rhetoric that they invited him to join. A few days later, he accepted.

So began one of the strangest political careers in recorded history. The German Workers Party had been founded a few months before as a front organization for the Thule Society, which was itself a front organization for another secret society, the Germanenorden Walvater. As Hitler took over the little party and began making it effective, others in the Thule Society took notice. The society's membership included many German aristocrats and intellectuals. They were able to see to it that the party got the funding and opportunities it needed. They also ensured that Hitler was surrounded by capable aides who could cope with his erratic habits and help him use his rhetorical powers to best advantage.

Rebranded the National Socialist German Workers' Party—a label that was promptly contracted by Germans to *Nazi*—and adorned with a variant of the Thule Society's swastika emblem, the party soon became a major force in German politics. As it grew, the Thule Society quietly shut down its other activities and put all its energies into its monstrous offspring.

SEE ALSO: The Germanenorden (1912), The Thule Society (1918), The SS (1925), Hitler Takes Power (1933)

A propaganda poster of the German People's Party, c. 1918–1921, published in Cologne, Germany, by M. DuMont Schauberg, The picture expresses the power of the new regime in the glorified form of an ironworker bearing down on an anvil, hammer poised.

PROHIBITION

ITS PROPONENTS CALLED IT THE GREAT Experiment and praised it as the next inevitable forward step in the march of moral progress. The main result of the prohibition of alcoholic beverages in the United States from 1920 to 1933, though, was an immense boost to organized crime, and above all to the Mafia, which had become well established in Italian American communities by the time Prohibition took effect.

Until Prohibition, the Mafia was only one of dozens of ethnic crime syndicates that found niches in American immigrant neighborhoods, providing illegal goods and services and cutting deals with corrupt city officials. The Mafia proved to be tougher and more violent than most of its rivals, though; within a few years it became the major purveyor of illegal liquor in most large American cities. The spectacular wealth to be gotten by smuggling and selling illegal liquor guaranteed the outbreak of violence between competing organized-crime groups. Assassinations, drive-by shootings, and mass murders became commonplace in the 1920s, and the news media of the time marketed lurid stories of gangland activities to the public.

Ironically, Prohibition also launched a very different secret society on its way. The Order of Camels was founded in Milwaukee, Wisconsin, in 1920. Its goal was to overturn Prohibition and make alcohol legal again in the United States. Its founding members chose the name because camels are legendary for being able to go a long time without a drink. The Order of Camels helped organize political pressure against Prohibition; they also engaged in smuggling operations. In 1933, once Prohibition was repealed, the Order of Camels quietly dissolved.

SEE ALSO: The Mafia Comes to America (c. 1880), Al Capone becomes *Capo dei Capi* (1929)

The humorous banner displayed in Daniel Hagerman's c. 1920 photo sums up the thinking of the Order of Camels, a Milwaukee-based lodge. The organization pledged its members to a campaign against Prohibition, with the goal of repealing the Eighteenth Amendment.

THE COMMITTEE OF 300

WALTER RATHENAU (1867–1922) WAS A leading financier and politician in Germany after World War I; he was also Jewish. In the hothouse atmosphere of the Weimar Republic, where the Nazi Party was only one of many flavors of the radical right, that was an explosive combination. When Rathenau mentioned in a 1921 book that the economic system of Europe was effectively under the control of three hundred men, that offhand remark launched a full-blown conspiracy panic.

Rathenau had said the same thing in a 1909 newspaper article without stirring up a furor, but in 1921 the first German translation of *The Protocols of the Elders of Zion* had just hit the bookshelves. German anti-Semites immediately pulled Rathenau's comment out of context, insisted that the three hundred men in question were the heads of the Jewish world conspiracy, and claimed that the fact that Rathenau knew the exact number proved that he was one of them. In 1922, as a direct result of this propaganda, Rathenau was assassinated by right-wing fanatics.

By the middle years of the twentieth century, the Committee of 300 had become a fixture of conspiracy literature in Europe; The group soon found its way across the Atlantic, where it appeared in literature sponsored by the John Birch Society. By century's end it had become part of the elaborate hierarchies that were fashionable among conspiracy researchers at that time. Ironically, although Rathenau was probably correct—the U.S. economy today is managed by about that number of important CEOs, financiers, and major investors—no evidence has ever been offered to show that any organized "Committee of 300" actually exists.

SEE ALSO: *The Protocols of the Elders of Zion* (1895), Hitler Takes Power (1933), The John Birch Society (1959), The New World Order (1991)

A photo of Walther Rathenau, German statesman and foreign minister during the Weimar Republic. Anti-Semites in Germany took Rathenau's comments about the "three hundred men," who presumably controlled the economic system in Europe at the time, out of context and launched a full-on anti-Semitic backlash that would result in Rathenau's death.

THE COUNCIL ON FOREIGN RELATIONS

IN THE WAKE OF WORLD WAR I, MEMBERS OF the industrial world's political and economic elite surveyed the wreckage and tried to find ways to keep any similar catastrophe from happening again. Some of the ventures launched as a result, such as the League of Nations, were highly public, but others inevitably pursued less obvious routes. One of these was the Council on Foreign Relations (CFR).

In 1919, at the Paris peace talks, Colonel Edward House (1858–1938)—a close adviser of U.S. president Woodrow Wilson (1856–1924)—met with an assortment of British and American politicians and proposed the creation of an institute to coordinate public policy among the English-speaking nations. The Council on Foreign Relations was accordingly founded in New York City two years later, in 1921; its British affiliate, the Royal Institute for International Affairs (RIAA), was founded in London in 1920. Both organizations recruited their membership from among the most important movers and shakers in politics, finance, business, and the academic sphere in their respective nations.

Neither the CFR nor the RIAA are, strictly speaking, secret societies—the CFR even publishes a bimonthly magazine, *Foreign Affairs*—but both have come to play a very large role in current conspiracy beliefs. The John Birch Society early on named the CFR as one of the core institutions in the sinister conspiracy of "insiders" it believed it was fighting. Current writings on the subject routinely identify the CFR, along with the Trilateral Commission, the Bilderbergers, and the Committee of 300, as the institutional forms currently taken by the Bavarian Illuminati.

SEE ALSO: The Bavarian Illuminati (1776), The Committee of 300 (1921), The John Birch Society (1959), *Trilateralism* (1980), The New World Order (1991)

A photo of Colonel Edward House, c. 1919. House, a close advisor to President Woodrow Wilson, played an important role in founding the Council on Foreign Relations.

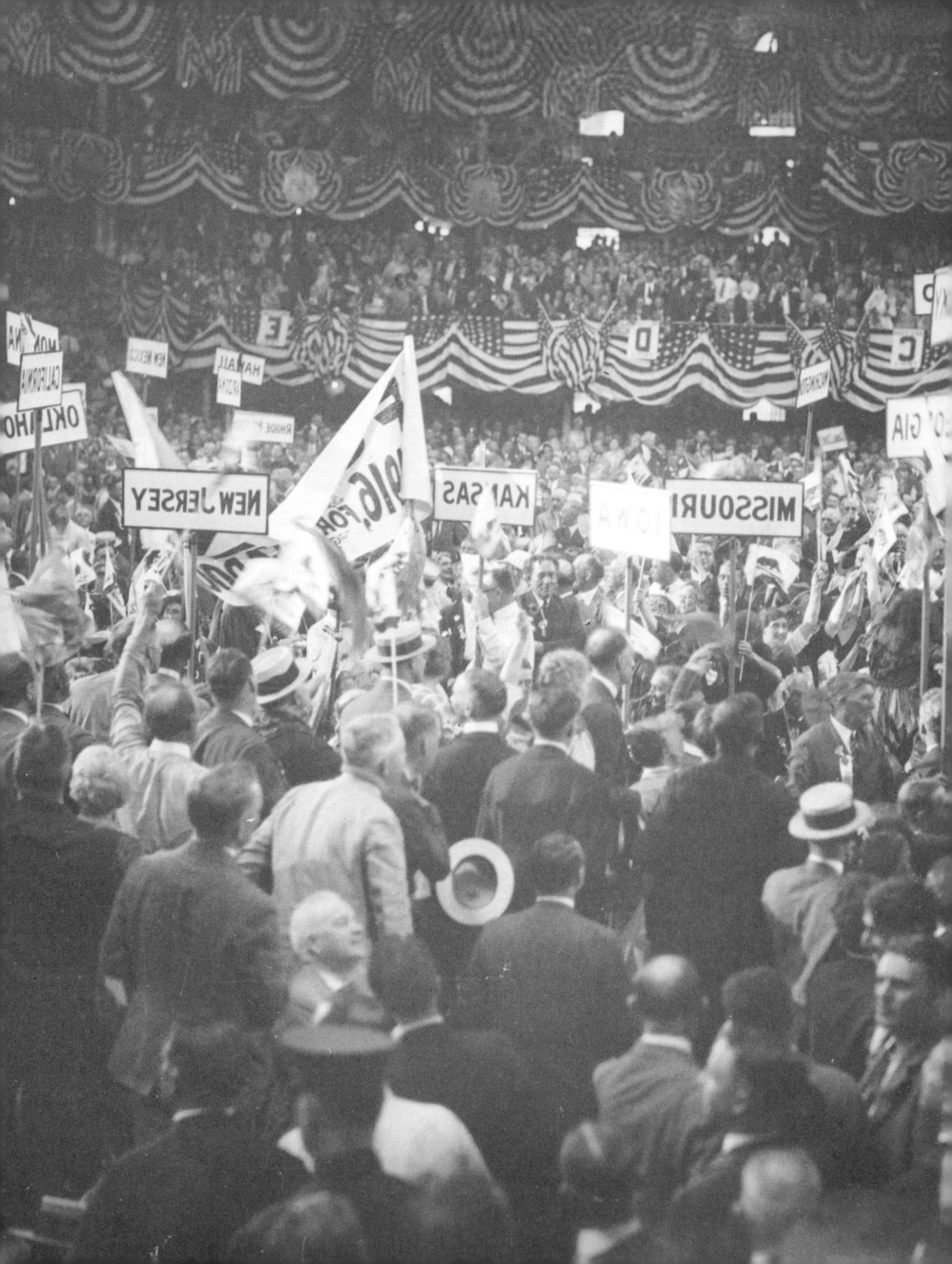
NEW JERSEY
KANSAS
IOWA
MISSOURI
CALIFORNIA

ANTI-KLAN SECRET SOCIETIES

BY 1923, THE REORGANIZED KU KLUX KLAN had become a significant presence in U.S. politics and culture. In response, many Americans who rejected the Klan's goals decided to fight fire with fire by founding anti-Klan secret societies.

There were at least four such organizations. All of them were founded in 1923, and each chose a different angle of attack. The All-American Association, borrowing the tactics of the American Protective League, set out to gather information on illegal Klan activities and inform the media and law enforcement. The Knights of Liberty, founded by an ex-Klansman driven out of the order for opposing its covert policy of violence, offered potential recruits an alternative that rejected all illegal activity. The picturesquely named Order of Anti-Poke-Noses was founded in Arkansas to oppose "any organization that attends to everyone's business but their own."

Then there was the Knights of the Flaming Circle, the largest and most colorful of the anti-Klan secret societies. Where the Klan required members to be white, male, Protestant, and native-born, the Knights of the Flaming Circle only enlisted people of color, women, members of other religions, and immigrants. Its members wore black robes, and they staged rallies as big as the Klan's to remind politicians and the public that the Klan did not speak for all Americans.

The anti-Klan secret societies flourished during the 1920s, and went out of existence after the revived Klan collapsed at the end of that decade. To this day, no one is sure just how large a role they played in bringing about the fall of the Klan, but it may have been considerable.

SEE ALSO: The Ku Klux Klan (1865), The Klan Reborn (1915), The American Protective League (1917), The Klan Destroyed (1925)

Secret societies that advocated the end of the Klan were supported by mainstream efforts from politicians such as Andrew Cobb Erwin (1884–1941), a delegate from Athens, Georgia. His stirring speech denouncing the Ku Klux Klan at the 1924 Democratic National Convention was met with deafening salvos of cheers and applause from the audience. The photo, left, shows an anti-Klan demonstration that took place later that evening following Erwin's speech at the convention.

RELUCTANCE !

THE SS

BY 1925, THE NAZI PARTY HAD BECOME large and influential enough that its leader, Adolf Hitler, began touring to drum up support. One danger presented itself: throughout the 1920s in Germany, far-right parties such as the Nazis, and far-left parties such as the Communists, routinely got into street brawls with each other and tried to break up each other's meetings. In response, the party organized a group of volunteer bodyguards to protect Hitler on his tours. They called it *der Schutzstaffel*, the Protection Squad, or simply the SS.

That's what it remained until 1929, when a series of political struggles put Heinrich Himmler (1900–1945), a colorless young man with the manners of a college professor, in charge of the SS. Himmler saw unexpected potentials in the small organization and went to Hitler with a daring proposal: he wanted to turn the SS into a semi-secret society within the Nazi Party, with its own initiation rituals, symbolism, and total personal loyalty to Hitler himself. Hitler gave his approval, and the SS transformed itself into one of the cornerstones of the future Nazi regime.

Membership in the SS was voluntary and only open to those who passed tests of racial purity. Most members held down day jobs and donned their black uniforms for local meetings once or twice a week, where they took part in military drills and attended lectures on Nazi political and racial theory. After the Nazis came to power in 1933, new SS branches—the Waffen-SS, a private army, and the Gestapo, the Nazi Party's secret police—were added to the structure. SS membership then turned into a career requirement for writers and intellectuals who wanted to get ahead under the new regime. It remained one of the pillars of the Nazi state until Germany's total defeat in World War II brought down the curtain on Himmler's dreams.

SEE ALSO: The Thule Society (1918), Hitler Takes Power (1933)

This satirical, anti-Nazi cartoon mocks Heinrich Himmler, commander of the SS, head of the Gestapo, and arguably the most ruthless man in Nazi Germany other than Adolf Hitler. It shows Himmler exerting, with "reluctance," the "murderous methods" that "only the British" might use, over Czechoslovakia, a country that Hitler first annexed and then occupied.

THE KLAN DESTROYED

BY 1925, THE REORGANIZED KU KLUX KLAN was riding high. It had successfully expanded out of the South, establishing itself on a huge scale in the Midwest and West and making inroads in New England and the Mid-Atlantic States; with millions of members and an ample treasury, it was reaching for political power. The Klan essentially ran the state of Indiana, where one out of four white adult men were Klan members, and the Grand Dragon of Indiana, David Stephenson, (1891–1966) was preparing to run for president in the 1928 elections.

In 1925, however, Stephenson abducted and raped his secretary. She took poison, but she lived long enough to talk to the police and the media. Stephenson was arrested and convicted of the crime, and the governor of Indiana, fearing a media backlash, refused to pardon him. Infuriated by this, Stephenson talked to the authorities, revealing a massive pattern of Klan illegalities and landing more than a dozen elected officials in jail.

The effect on the Klan was catastrophic. Faced with a media firestorm aided and abetted by the efforts of anti-Klan secret societies, most Klansmen quit the order, and nearly all Klaverns outside the South went out of existence in the second half of the 1920s. In the 1930s, the Klan handed an even more devastating weapon to its opponents by allying with the German-American Bund and other pro-Nazi groups. As the United States aligned with Britain in the run-up to World War II, the Klan lost most of its remaining members. In 1944, faced with a bill for more than half a million dollars in back taxes, the Knights of the Ku Klux Klan dissolved. While Klan groups remain active to this day, none of them has a fraction of the Klan's former power.

SEE ALSO: The Ku Klux Klan (1865), The Klan Reborn (1915), Anti-Klan Secret Societies (1923)

A portrait of former Ku Klux Klan Grand Dragon of Indiana, David Stephenson, on trial for the rape and murder of Madge Oberholtzer in 1925. Stephenson's conviction and subsequent revelations about other illegal Klan activities had a profound effect on the dissolution of the Klan's power in most parts of the United States other than the South.

OPUS DEI

ALL THROUGH ITS HISTORY, THE ROMAN Catholic Church has been shaped by struggles between the central authority of the pope and the local churches and monastic orders under his authority. In those struggles, popes have repeatedly turned for support to Catholic religious bodies that were outside the authority of local bishops. The Knights Templar and the Jesuits each occupied that role in their time; currently, the organization that serves the same function is Opus Dei.

The Prelature of the Holy Cross and Opus Dei, to give it its full name, was founded by Spanish priest Josemaría Escrivá de Balaguer (1902–1975) in 1928 as an association for Catholic laypersons. Its relationship with the Vatican has varied as one pope gave way to another, but in 1982 Pope John Paul II (1920–2005) gave it the status of "personal prelature," freeing its members and activities from supervision by local bishops and church officials. In 2002, its founder was canonized as a saint.

Highly secretive and disciplined, Opus Dei has some 85,000 members, a quarter of whom are wholly committed to the organization, live in houses it owns, and donate all their earnings to it. Church officials speak glowingly of the association, and defend its traditional attitudes toward sexuality and obedience. Its critics, including a large number of ex-members, describe it as a cult-like secret society with a right-wing political agenda. To judge from the earlier organizations that had the same role in Catholicism, the truth probably lies somewhere between these two extremes.

SEE ALSO: Fall of the Knights Templar (1307)

Josemaría Escrivá de Balaguer, founder of Opus Dei, is pictured here, c. 1965, preaching to an enthusiastic crowd. Josemaría Escrivá was canonized on October 6, 2002, only twenty-seven years after his death in 1975. It was one of the shortest waiting periods in Church history. An estimated 300,000 people filled St. Peter's Square for the canonization.

AL CAPONE BECOMES
CAPO DEI CAPI

IN THE WAKE OF PROHIBITION, THE CHRONIC warfare between competing organized-crime syndicates in the United States went into overdrive. The immense profits to be made from smuggling and selling illegal liquor fueled bitter struggles to control local markets—struggles that typically involved plenty of gunfire and a large body count.

That changed because of a man named Alphonse Capone (1899–1947). An outsider by Mafia standards—he was born in Rome, not the traditional Mafia stronghold of Sicily—he clawed his way to the top of the Mafia hierarchy in Chicago, then brokered a truce among the competing Italian, Irish, Jewish, and Polish gangs that had a share in Chicago's bootleg-liquor trade. Each gang received exclusive control over specific territories in the city and cooperated with other gangs in arranging shipments of liquor and evading law enforcement. The results were so profitable for all concerned that in 1929 Capone arranged for a convention of organized-crime heads in Atlantic City, New Jersey, where a similar scheme was set up for the United States as a whole, with Capone as *Capo dei Capi*, America's number one mobster.

Capone's truce lasted until he was jailed on tax-evasion charges in 1931. In his absence, renewed warfare broke out among competing gangs, but the struggle came to an end as Charles "Lucky" Luciano (1897–1962)—the leading figure in the younger generation of Mafiosi—had his opponents gunned down and reestablished Capone's system with himself as *Capo dei Capi*. With the help of his right-hand man, Jewish mobster Meyer Lansky (1902–1983), Luciano forced a permanent peace on the quarrelsome Mafia clans, establishing a system that remains in place today.

SEE ALSO: The Mafia Comes to America (c.1880), Prohibition (1920)

After serving a one-year sentence for gun possession at Eastern State Penitentiary, Al Capone looks happy in this photo, as he fishes off the stern of his boat moored near his Florida mansion. Capone would be back in jail again one year later (in 1931) on a rap for tax evasion, which would keep him behind bars for the next eleven years.

HITLER TAKES POWER

As the Great Depression spread across the industrial world, the fragile democracies of central Europe cracked under the strain. The Nazi Party was well placed to take advantage of the crisis. Germany was still reeling from the economic burdens of the Versailles Treaty; many Germans longed for the stability and prosperity of the imperial regime, and many more were profoundly worried about the rising strength of the German Communist Party. Hitler toured the country, making speech after speech that promised better times to come. As the crisis deepened and the government did nothing effective to counteract it, the Nazi Party grew rapidly.

Despite this, the 1932 elections saw the Nazi Party fall well short of a majority. Hoping to hijack the new party's popularity for their own ends, a cabal of conservative politicians offered Hitler the office of chancellor (a position that was at that time normally appointed by the president and was a comparatively weak office) in a coalition government. Hitler accepted, and then turned the tables on his supposed allies, using his own popularity and his party's strong-arm tactics to push a series of laws through the Reichstag that gave the chancellor's office unlimited power.

Among the edicts that followed, as Hitler remade Germany in the Nazi image, was one outlawing Freemasonry and all other secret societies, including Ariosophical orders. Having begun his road to power using secret-society methods, Hitler clearly meant to stop anyone else from using the same strategies against his regime. The Ariosophical orders that had shaped the Nazi movement were prohibited along with all others. The SS promptly took their place and seized a central role in German society, which it kept until the Thousand-Year Reich imploded 988 years ahead of schedule.

SEE ALSO: The Thule Society (1918), The SS (1925), Neo-Nazi Secret Societies (1945)

A Nazi propaganda poster featuring a glorified image of Adolf Hitler, surrounded by a few of the most potent symbols of the Third Reich. Other posters, like this one, were emblazoned with nationalist slogans such as *"Es Lebe Deutschland"* (Long live Germany).

THE CAGOULE

Germany was far from the only European country that faced the threat of organized fascist movements in the troubled decade of the 1930s. The failure of democratic governments to cope effectively with the Great Depression gave encouragement to nationalist radicals. In France, the most colorful of these had a cumbersome name: the Secret Organization of National Revolutionary Action. Its members adopted, from the Ku Klux Klan in America, the habit of wearing pointed hoods to conceal their identities, and so the organization came to be known publicly as *"le Cagoule,"* French for "the hood."

The Cagoule was founded in 1935 by Eugène Deloncle (1890–1944), and quickly attracted a large following among French reactionaries. It was organized along military lines and received aid from the fascist regimes in Italy, Germany, and Spain, importing large quantities of weapons for the planned coup. Meanwhile the Cagoule carried out the usual projects of espionage and infiltration, and finally set out to discredit France's left-wing movement by staging a series of false-flag bombings of business organizations in Paris in September 1937.

Unfortunately for the Cagoule's ambitions, the authorities figured out promptly who was behind the bombings. Deloncle was arrested a month later, and shortly thereafter police located the Cagoule's arms caches. The organization was quickly crushed after the German conquest of France in 1940; many of its members went on to collaborate with the Nazis and the Vichy puppet government they installed over France.

SEE ALSO: The Klan Reborn (1915), Hitler Takes Power (1933)

This photo, taken in 1938, shows only a fraction of the Cagoule's arsenal, seized by French authorities after the organization's leader, Eugène Deloncle, was arrested in the fall of 1937.

WILHELM LANDIG

Rebellen für

THULE

NEO-NAZI SECRET SOCIETIES

THE TWELVE-YEAR REICH OF NAZI Germany was a resounding failure even by the standards it set for itself, but the twisted charisma of Hitler's regime continued to attract followers even after the Führer's charred corpse was hauled out of a Berlin bunker. Widespread public revulsion that followed the revelation of the Nazi regime's crimes, backed up in many countries by laws against Nazi activities, made secret societies a logical choice for those followers; so, from 1945 on, a profusion of neo-Nazi secret societies came into being in Europe and elsewhere.

Like the secret societies that launched the Nazi movement in the first place, many of the neo-Nazi secret societies had a strong occult element. Elaborate mythologies involving the lost continent of Thule, the hollow earth, flying saucers, and other galaxies were invented to explain away the Third Reich's total failure and claim the imminent arrival of a glorious Aryan future. Such ideas were central to the work of Wilhelm Landig, (1909–1997) a Viennese writer and occultist who seems to have launched the first neo-Nazi secret society immediately after the war, and were picked up and reworked by more influential authors such as Savitri Devi (1905–1982), Miguel Serrano (1917–2009), and the colorful James H. Madole (1927–1979) of the American Renaissance Party.

For the first few decades after the war, the emerging neo-Nazi underground focused on such themes, just as the old Ariosophical secret societies had done in the early twentieth century. Not until a new generation of radicals entered the movement were there again attempts to put neo-Nazi ideology into practice through revolutionary violence.

SEE ALSO: Ariosophy (1908), The Thule Society (1918), The American Renaissance Party (1949), The Order (1983)

The cover of the novel _Rebellen für Thule—Das Erbe von Atlantis_ (Rebels for Thule—the inheritance from Atlantis). The book is part of a trilogy published by Wilhelm Landig, beginning in the late 1930s, and which is still in print. Landig's books explore the mythologies of the lost continent of Thule. These stories became articles of faith for many neo-Nazi secret societies after the collapse of the Nazi regime in 1945.

Il Fascista:

LICIO GELLI

di Ettore

Ricopre l'incarico:
Ispettore Nazionale
Organizzazione Fasci
Combattimento Estero

DIRETTORIO CENTRALE

Data 23 Maggio 1941

Le autorità sono invitate a soddisfare ogni forma di assistenza richiesta.

Posizione n. 23 375-P-D.

Sez. 42-RR-PT-573

Il Funzionario

PROPAGANDA DUE (P2)

ITALY IN THE WAKE OF WORLD WAR II WAS a battleground between Fascist and Communist factions. Most Italian Freemasons tried to stay out of the crossfire, but there were exceptions, and one of them was Licio Gelli (1919–2015). In the late 1960s, he became head of an unofficial Masonic lodge in Rome named *Propaganda Due* ("Propaganda 2"), or P2 for short, and turned it into a political secret society on the far right of Italian politics.

P2 had a complex history. It had originally been founded by the Masonic Grand Lodge of Italy in 1877, as a secret lodge for members of Italy's parliament who wanted to become Masons, while keeping their membership secret from the Catholic Church. Suppressed in 1924, it was revived in 1946 and quickly attracted many right-wing Italian politicians. Senior Mafiosi also joined, and so—despite the Church's official ban on Masonry—did officials from the Vatican.

P2 received money from the CIA to fight Communism, although the evidence suggests that Gelli played the CIA and KGB against each other, took money from both, and pocketed it. Gelli and other P2 members also helped broker an arrangement between the Vatican and the Mafia, by which the Vatican bank laundered money for the Mafia and took a cut of the proceeds. All this came out in 1981, after the collapse of the financial empire of P2 member Michele Sindona (1920–1986), which brought a police investigation. As the sordid details of P2's financial and political machinations became front-page news, several leading P2 members—including Sindona and Gelli—suddenly died or disappeared. P2 officially went out of existence, though rumors continue to spread that it has simply been restarted under another name.

SEE ALSO: *In Eminente* (1738)

1946

Licio Gelli's ID dating from 1941, when he was a functionary of Benito Mussolini's fascist government. Gelli continued as a player in sordid right-wing politics in Italy, including laundering Mafia money through the Vatican. This 1941 ID is just one of many artifacts of Gelli's life that make his eventual downfall seem like a foregone conclusion. At a news conference in 1999, Gelli reportedly said, "I am a fascist and will die a fascist."

THE MAU MAUS

1948

THE SAME REVOLUTIONARY ASPIRATIONS that shook Europe in the nineteenth century flowered anew in the Third World in the twentieth, as indigenous peoples demanded independence from European colonial rule. Most of those struggles were straightforward rebellions, often with a veneer of Marxism to attract financial aid and arms from the Soviet Union, but in some cases the classic methods of conspiracy were put to use once again in the quest for freedom.

That was what happened in the British colony of Kenya, where the Kikuyu people formed a secret society, the Movement of Unity, to stop the expropriation of Kikuyu land by white farmers and drive out the colonial government. White settlers and colonial officials called the movement the *Mau Maus*, a garbling of the Kikuyu words *Uma uma*, "Out! Out!"—the warning cry that told members to scatter when the police raided a meeting.

Protest marches and legal appeals did nothing to advance the movement's goals. Guerrilla war was the next logical step; by 1951, rural guerrilla forces were active all through the mountains of Kenya, supported by an urban wing in the large cities that provided support and intelligence. Meanwhile the Kenyan African Union, the political arm of the movement, continued to press for change using legal means.

In 1952, a state of emergency was declared by the British colonial government; British Army units tried to crush the rising, with limited success. Four years later, facing yet another unwinnable guerrilla war, Britain bowed to the inevitable and began the process of devolution that ended in Kenya's independence seven years later. The methods of the Fenian Brotherhood had proven just as effective in Africa as in Ireland.

SEE ALSO: The Easter Rising (1916)

When the British colonial government in Kenya declared a state of emergency in 1952, troops of the King's African Rifles, like the armed soldiers seen in this photo taken c. 1952–1956, took part in operations against the Mau Maus. A Kikuyu secret society, the Mau Maus aimed to kick out the colonial government and put an end to Britain's land grab in Kenya.

"AMERICA FIRST" rally.... in Yorkville

AMERICANS AWAKE! RAISE HIGH THE BANNER OF AMERICAN NATIONALISM AND RACIAL PRIDE! The National
Renaissance Party has returned to Yorkville in order to mobilize the strength of American patrio
who supported the dynamic fighting principles of men like Father Charles Coughlin of the Christi
Front, Charles Lindberg of the America First Party, the late Senator Joseph McCarthy, General
Douglas MacArthur, and Major General Edwin Walker. THE NRP WISHES TO REGAIN THE LOST "CIVIL
RIGHTS" OF THE WHITE CHRSTIAN MAJORITY OF THE AMERICAN PEOPLE.

Are you aware that well organized racial minority groups have succeeded in banning Christian
prayer, Christmas carols, and all forms of Christian religious observances in the public schools
of the United States? Are you aware that these same groups are now planning to outlaw both the
Pledge of Allegiance and the Lord's Prayer from our public schools in order to kill the last
vestiges of patriotism and Christian moral concepts in the minds of your children? J. Edgar
Hoover of the FBI admits that the rate of crime, narcotics addiction, and teen-age prostitution
has zoomed upwards during the past few years BUT HOOVER LIKE OTHER AMERICAN POLITICIANS, DARES
NOT TO ASSOCIATE THE UPWARD SPIRAL OF CRIME AND JUVENILE DELINQUENCY WITH THE CHANGING RACIAL
COMPLEXION OF THE UNITED STATES AND THE FORCED RACIAL INTEGRATION OF OUR PUBLIC SCHOOLS! Are
you aware that forced integration of public schools brings White children into daily intimate
contact with youthful members of more primitive racial groups AND THAT THE UNDESIREABLE NAR-
COTICS HABITS AND SEXUAL PROMISCUITY OF THESE MORE PRIMITIVE RACIAL GROUPS ARE BOUND TO RUB OFF
ON THEIR WHITE ASSOCIATES? WHAT SINISTER FORCE HAS DIRECTED THE TERRIBLE CAMPAIGN OF SLANDER,
VILIFICATION, AND HATRED AGAINST THE GERMANIC PEOPLE FOR NEARLY THIRTY YEARS IN AMERICA'S "KEPT"
PRESS, RADIO, AND TV? WHO IS BEHIND THE PLOT TO KEEP GERMANY A DIVIDED NATION?

FOR THE ANSWER TO THESE AND OTHER VITAL QUESTIONS CONCERNING OUR SURVIVAL AS A NATION WE URGE
YOU TO ATTEND A MASS MEETING OF THE NRP AT THE FOLLOWING TIME AND PLACE:

TIME AND PLACE---THE MASS MEETING OF THE NATIONAL RENAISSANCE PARTY WILL TAKE PLACE ON FRIDAY
                 EVENING, JANUARY 11, 1963, AT 8 P.M., IN THE ATLAS ROOM OF THE YORKVILLE LABOR
                 TEMPLE, 157 EAST 86TH STREET, NYC. (THE BUILDING IS LOCATED NEAR THE AUTOMAT, BE-
                 TWEEN LEXINGTON & THIRD AVENUES. EASILY ACCESSIBLE BY IRT SUBWAY OR BUS.)

SPEAKERS--- FREDERICK E. JONES, FORMER U.S. MARINE, WILL SERVE AS CHAIRMAN AND SPEAK ON THE
            TOPIC OF "THE PAST AND PRESENT GOALS OF THE NRP IN YORKVILLE". THIS INCLUDES OUR
            PART IN DEFEATING LEFT-WING CANDIDATE, MARK LANE, IN 1961.

            JAMES H. MADOLE, NATIONAL DIRECTOR OF THE NRP, WHO WAS BANNED FROM TV AND RADIO IN
            1957 AS A RESULT OF HIS EXPOSURE OF THE SEDITIOUS ACTIVITIES OF MINORITY GROUP
            ORGANIZATIONS, WILL SPEAK ON "A DYNAMIC PROGRAM FOR THE REBIRTH OF AMERICAN NATIONAL-
            ISM".

            WALTER BRADLEY WILL SPEAK ON "THE MYTH OF RACIAL EQUALITY".

There will be martial music, pageantry, vast quantities of literature and information. Don't
hide like a craven coward while your country is destroyed from within. Make up a party of
friends. DON'T LET US DOWN. COMMUNISTS AND RACE-MIXING OUTFITS CAN PACK THEIR HALLS AND THUS
WIN POLITICAL VICTORIES. YOUR COWARDICE INSURES THEIR SUCCESS. FOR FURTHER INFORMATION AND
SAMPLE LITERATURE CONTACT: NATIONAL RENAISSANCE PARTY, 10 WEST 90TH STREET, NEW YORK 24, N.Y.

THE NATIONAL RENAISSANCE PARTY

PLENTY OF SCIENCE FICTION FANS IN MID-twentieth-century America dabbled in occultism and radical politics, but few of them had as great an impact on extremist politics as James H. Madole (1927–1979). A lifelong New Yorker, Madole got involved in science-fiction fandom in his early teens and drifted into the fascist end of science fiction in the 1940s. In 1945, as an eighteen-year-old, Madole founded a political party, the Animist Party, which drew nearly all its tiny membership from his fellow science-fiction fans. In 1949, Kurt Meurtig, a veteran pro-Nazi organizer, founded the National Renaissance Party, recruited Madole, and shortly thereafter made him the party's leader. Madole kept that position until his death thirty years later.

He was never just a Hitler copycat. He pioneered the "Third Way" economic theory that later became a staple of neo-fascist parties worldwide, rejecting socialism and capitalism alike in favor of a system modeled on the "corporatist state" of Mussolini's Italy. Like many other neo-Nazi thinkers in the postwar era, he mixed plenty of occultism with his fascism. He proposed the creation of a new human species, the "God-Man," through selective breeding, positive thinking, intensive training, and occult initiation.

Madole became a familiar figure on the far right in the postwar decades, lecturing in a buttoned-up suit, black horn-rimmed glasses, and a white motorcycle helmet. Despite his eccentricity, he played a major role in launching the neo-Nazi underground in North America. He died of cancer in 1979. His party collapsed almost immediately afterward, leaving the field clear for a new generation of neo-Nazi secret societies.

SEE ALSO: Neo-Nazi Secret Societies (1945)

This flyer, sponsored by the National Renaissance Party (NRP), advertises an "America First" rally to be held in the Atlas Room of the Yorkville Labor Temple at 157 East 86th Street in New York City at 8:00 p.m., on January 11, 1963. The opening salvo encapsulates the organization's credo: "Americans awake! Raise high the banner of American Nationalism and racial pride!" Note that one of the speakers at the meeting was to be NRP leader James H. Madole, who, according to the NRP, "was banned from TV and radio in 1957 as a result of his exposure of the seditious activities of minority group organizations."

THE BILDERBERGERS

IN THE WAKE OF WORLD WAR II, A GREAT many people argued that the only way to avoid an even worse catastrophe than that conflict in the future was to make sure that political and economic leaders in the world's industrial nations had plenty of opportunities to discuss the issues of the day out of the glare of publicity. Prince Bernhard of the Netherlands (1911–2004), a supporter of these views, accordingly organized an annual meeting of movers and shakers, which first met in the posh Bilderberg Hotel in Oosterbeek, the Netherlands, in 1954.

To the American far right in the overheated atmosphere of the 1950s, any meeting of this sort amounted to waving the proverbial red cloth at an already-enraged bull. The John Birch Society and other far-right U.S. groups such as the Liberty Lobby pounced on the meeting as proof of the vast conspiracy of "insiders." John Birch Society founder Robert Welch (1899–1985) identified them as secret puppet masters who ran the world, with links reaching back to the Bavarian Illuminati.

The meeting has moved elsewhere since the mid-1950s; it has been held in five-star hotels in an assortment of cities in Europe and the eastern seaboard of North America. Nevertheless, its identity in conspiracy literature has been fixed as "the Bilderberg Society," or simply "the Bilderbergers." That identification with the Dutch city continued straight through the great transformation of conspiracy theory in the 1970s, when beliefs that had been the property of the U.S. far right became widely accepted on the far left as well. To date, though, no one has offered any evidence that "the Bilderbergers" are more than an annual meeting of the influential.

SEE ALSO: The Bavarian Illuminati (1776), The Council on Foreign Relations (1921), The John Birch Society (1959), *Trilateralism* (1980)

A photo of Prince Bernhard of the Netherlands, c. 1944. With his global contacts, Bernhard organized a meeting at the Bilderberg Hotel in the Netherlands in May 1954. He brought together Western intellectuals and the business elite to discuss economic issues and, as some feared, the growing threat from Communism.

THE PRIORY OF SION

PIERRE PLANTARD (1920–2000) WANTED to be a big name in secret-society circles, and eventually he got his wish. As a teenager, he dabbled in reactionary politics and studied with Georges Monti, a small-time player in the Paris occult scene. In 1940, he launched his first secret society, Alpha Galates, with himself as Druidic Majesty; he later worked as a church janitor in Paris and studied the correspondence course issued by AMORC, a California-based Rosicrucian order. In 1956 he tried again, founding the Priory of Sion, and started claiming it was much larger than it was in order to boost paid memberships, a habit for which he did six months in jail for fraud.

Around this same time, he came up with a brilliant plan for giving his order a more impressive pedigree than it actually had. He and a friend began concocting forged documents about the Priory of Sion, and smuggled them into several important French libraries, which were accustomed to people trying to take documents out but had failed to anticipate that anyone would try to bring them in. Once they were in place, Plantard—who by then had tacked "de St.-Clair" on his name to sound more aristocratic—"discovered" and publicized his own inventions.

This all failed to attract many members to the Priory of Sion, but it did interest Henry Lincoln, Michael Baigent, and Richard Leigh, three British filmmakers who produced three BBC documentaries and a bestselling book, *The Holy Blood and the Holy Grail*, based on Plantard's fabrications. These same inventions later helped inspire Dan Brown's hugely popular novel *The Da Vinci Code*, which saw print three years after Plantard's death. In this way Plantard became the father of the most successful secret-society hoax since Leo Taxil's "Palladian Order."

SEE ALSO: The Rosicrucians (1614), The "Palladian Order" Hoax (1897)

A nineteenth-century print depicting Godfrey of Bouillon (1060–1100) being cheered by crusaders in Jerusalem. Godfrey, a Frankish knight, led the first crusade. Pierre Plantard claimed that the Priory of Sion was descended from a secret society that Godfrey supposedly founded in Jerusalem on Mount Zion.

TRUTH IS
OUR ONLY
WEAPON !!
WHAT'S YOURS,
TENG ?
THE JOHN BIRCH SOCIETY
CHAMBLEE - DORAVILLE
TAIWAN

THE JOHN BIRCH SOCIETY

EVEN IN THE MOST PARANOID ERAS, THERE are those who think that no one else is paranoid enough, and the United States in the red-baiting 1950s was no exception. No matter how frantically politicians and the media tried to find Communists under every bed, a hard-core fringe on the far right insisted that their slackness proved that they were Communist dupes. That fringe finally found its enduring voice in 1959, courtesy of Robert Welch Jr. (1899–1985).

Welch was a successful businessman who became convinced that America's political, economic, and cultural institutions were crawling with Communist agents. In 1959, using his business connections, he invited influential conservatives to a series of seminars, where he urged them to join him in founding a new organization to lobby for sterner measures against the Red threat. A name for the new society was provided by John Birch (1918–1945), a Baptist missionary in China killed by the Communists in 1945, whom Welch considered the first casualty of the Cold War.

The John Birch Society grew rapidly in its first years, with 16,000 members by the end of 1960, but it soon came under fire not only from liberals but from less extreme conservatives as well. Welch and his supporters responded by convincing themselves that capitalism, no less than Communism, was controlled by a sinister conspiracy of "insiders" descended from the Bavarian Illuminati, seeking to impose a new world order on the world, using tactics borrowed from the *Protocols of the Elders of Zion*. These beliefs proved too extreme for many of the society's members, but the organization survived the resulting downturn and remains active today.

SEE ALSO: The Bavarian Illuminati (1776), *The Protocols of the Elders of Zion* (1895), The New World Order (1991)

After its heyday in the 1960s, the John Birch Society is still active in the United States, and ever watchful of the Communist agenda, as they see it. That preoccupation is evident in this AP photo, taken on February 1, 1979. It shows members of the John Birch Society, the American Party, and fundamentalist Christian and pro-Taiwan groups protesting the visit of Deng Xiaoping (1904–1997), China's senior deputy prime minister, to Atlanta, Georgia.

THE CLUB OF ROME

AS THE TWENTIETH CENTURY DREW ON, the concern with international politics that inspired the birth of the Council on Foreign Relations, the Bilderbergers, and other elite organizations began to give way to broader concerns that industrial civilization itself might be unsustainable. One response to this was an organization founded in 1968 by Aurelio Peccei (1908–1984), a former CEO of the Fiat automobile firm, and a circle of industrialists and social scientists. The Club of Rome, as their organization was called, focused on what Peccei called "the global problematique"— the widening mismatch between limitless economic growth and the limited resources of a small planet.

The Club of Rome's most famous project was a study of the future of industrial society carried out by a team of computer scientists at MIT, and published in 1972 as *The Limits to Growth*. It ignited a media firestorm, as politicians and the general public alike objected to its claim that infinite growth on a finite planet was a recipe for disaster. Subsequent research projects funded by the Club of Rome, which tried to propose solutions for the problematique, attracted little attention.

With the coming of the 1980s, conservative parties in Europe and America abandoned the focus on sustainability and environmental protection that played so large a role in the politics of the previous decade. One consequence of this shift is that conspiracy theorists on the rightward end of the political spectrum redefined the Club of Rome and other environmental organizations as conspiracies. Ironically, that redefinition has remained in place even as the problems predicted in *The Limits to Growth* appear on the front pages of newspapers around the world.

SEE ALSO: The Council on Foreign Relations (1921), The Bilderbergers (1954)

A photo of Aurelio Peccei, founder of the Club of Rome, taken in October 1976. Peccei's predictions, dating back to 1968, about the impact of unlimited economic growth on global resources and the environment, were alarmingly prescient.

TRILATERALISM

U NTIL THE LAST QUARTER OF THE TWENTI-
eth century, conspiracy beliefs in
America flourished mostly in right-
wing political circles. The long tradition
of American conservative populism that
produced the Anti-Masonic Party, the Know-
Nothing Party, the American Protective
Association, and the John Birch Society had
a dominant position in conspiracy research,
and most people on the left ridiculed the
claim that secret societies had any influence
on society as a whole.

In the wake of the 1960s, though, many
people on the left were profoundly disap-
pointed by the failure of the radical movements of those years to achieve their political
and social goals. A large number of radicals
were unsatisfied by Marxist explanations of
that failure, and turned to conspiracy beliefs
instead, borrowing ideas wholesale from
the John Birch Society and other right-wing
groups but putting their own political slant
on the resulting claims.

The turning point in this process came in
1980, when Holly Sklar's (b. 1955) widely read
book *Trilateralism* was published. Sklar focused
on the Trilateral Commission, a rival to the
Council on Foreign Relations founded in 1973
by banker David Rockefeller (1915 2017) and
policy wonk Zbigniew Brzezinski (1928–2017),
and her book accepted most of the claims about
sinister "insiders" made a generation before by
John Birch Society founder Robert Welch.

Sklar's book became to modern left-wing
conspiracy research what Robison's *Proofs
of a Conspiracy* had been to conservatism
in the wake of the French Revolution. Like
Robison's book, it legitimized conspiracy as
an explanation for unwanted social change
and made secret societies a topic of discussion all through a movement that had previously been uninterested in it.

SEE ALSO: Skull and Bones (1832), The Council on
Foreign Relations (1921), The New World Order (1991)

David Rockefeller, then head of Chase Manhattan Bank and founder of the Trilateral Commission (in 1973), is seen here with Japan's Takeshi Watanabe (1906–1910), a chairman of the commission, speaking with reporters during a press conference on June 14, 1978. The economic group had been meeting in Washington, DC, for several days. Conspiracy theorists on both the right and left wing of American politics believed that the Trilateral Commission was intent on creating a worldwide economic power greater than the governments and nations involved. They also thought that the commission, as creators of the system, would "rule the future," as then senator Barry Goldwater put it so succinctly.

THE ORDER

ROBERT MATHEWS (1953–1984) WASN'T willing to sit still any more. A passionate member of the neo-Nazi underground in America, with connections all through the radical right, he was convinced that a race war was brewing, pitting racially pure Aryans against people of color, Jews, and white liberals. In 1983, after reading race-war novel *The Turner Diaries*, by William Pierce (1953–1984), he decided to put Pierce's fictional scenario into practice, and organized a secret society, the Order, to launch a campaign of terrorism against ZOG, the so-called Zionist Occupation Government of the United States.

Mathews found eager recruits among members of other neo-Nazi groups who were tired of the armchair theorists who dominated the radical right at that time, and wanted to see action. Once the organization was well established, following the scenario in Pierce's novel, Order members carried out an armored-car robbery and counterfeited U.S. currency to raise money for the coming struggle. They also assassinated Alan Berg, a Jewish talk-show host who made a habit of baiting racists on his radio shows.

These actions brought down a massive response from law enforcement. The FBI had little difficulty placing an undercover agent in the group, and raids followed. Mathews was cornered in a safe house on Whidbey Island, Washington, and died in a hail of bullets, while most of the other members of the organization were rounded up and sentenced to multiple life terms in federal prisons. With these arrests, the order effectively ceased to exist, and the rest of the neo-Nazi underground quietly abandoned any further plans it had for armed struggle.

SEE ALSO: Neo-Nazi Secret Societies (1945)

U.S. Marshals armed with automatic weapons stand guard at the Federal Courthouse in Denver, October 27, 1987, as four members of the neo-Nazi group the Order arrive for the second day of their trial in connection with the killing of radio talk show host Alan Berg.

fers, means "infiltration" then the fact that probably twenty times as many U.S.A. Presbyterian ministers have likewise transferred to the Southern Church means 20 times as much infiltration.

Then we challenge the expression, "for ulterior and subversive purposes." The Orthodox Presbyterian Church is concerned for the gospel as set forth in Scripture, for the historical faith including the so-called "Fundamentals," for the Presbyterianism and Calvinism of the Westminster Confession. If a concern to promote this is "ulterior and subversive" of what the Outlook wants for the Southern Church, then the Southern Church had better get rid of the Outlook (or the men who publish it, as it is an independent paper.). To the best of our knowledge, no minister has ever gone from the Orthodox Presbyterian Church to any other denomination, with the leaders of the Orthodox Presbyterian Church wanting him to be anything other than loyal to the historic Presbyterian faith. Do the leaders of the Southern Church want it to be a "Presbyterian" Church, or not?

Finally, we regret the expression contained in the closing paragraph of the report—'let bygones be bygones, and close ranks to press forward with mutual respect and confidence . . .' If this means, as it seems to mean, that the Liberals and the Conservatives in the Southern Church should forget their differences and cooperate for the general advance of the Church then the Conservatives, at least, have forgotten that the Church exists for the promotion of the gospel, not for self-preservation. And to lose the "first love" is to bring one's self under the condemnation of Christ.

L. W. S.

Solis Installed in San Francisco Church

Mr. Salvador M. Solis, a graduate of Westminster Seminary in 1957, was ordained to the gospel ministry and installed as pastor of First Orthodox Presbyterian Church of San Francisco at a service held at 1823 Turk Street on Friday, May 23.

Participating in the service were ministers Henry Coray of Sunnyvale, Richard Lewis of Berkeley, Lionel Brown of Covenant Church, R. J. Rushdoony of Santa Cruz, and Mr. Arthur Riffel of Brentwood Church.

Before coming to San Francisco, Mr. Solis did evangelistic work for the Christian Reformed Church in Modesto. He was born in Montery, California, and attended San Jose State College.

Westminster Faculty Members in Europe

Three members of the Westminster Seminary faculty are spending some time in Europe this summer.

Professor John Murray is vacationing in Scotland with relatives.

Professor Edward J. Young is on a lecture tour which includes stops in England, N. Ireland, and Germany. He was to return to this country on July 23.

Professor Ned B. Stonehouse left on July 7 on a trip which includes various stops on the continent, and then attendance at the Reformed Ecumenical Synod in South Africa. He planned to attend meetings of the International Association for Reformed Faith and Action in Strasbourg, France the latter part of July, the Reformed Ecumenical Synod in Potchefstroom, S. Africa August 6-15, and meetings of the Studiorum Novi Testamenti Societas, again in Strasbourg, September 2-5. He expects to arrive back in this country September 7.

A Wedding and Two Engagements

On Saturday, June 21 Mr. Bernard Stonehouse, son of Professor Ned B. Stonehouse of Westminster Seminary, and Miss Katherine C. Hunt, daughter of the Rev. and Mrs. Bruce F. Hunt, were united in marriage at Calvary Orthodox Presbyterian Church of Glenside, Pa. The ceremony was performed by Dr. Stonehouse, assisted by Mr. Hunt. Mr. and Mrs. Stonehouse will be completing academic work at Calvin College during the coming year.

Dr. and Mrs. Edward J. Young of Willow Grove, Pa., have announced the engagement of their daughter, Jean M. to Richard B. Gaffin Jr., son of the Rev. and Mrs. Richard Gaffin of Formosa. The wedding is to take place August 23. Mr. Gaffin will be attending Westminster Seminary this coming year.

The Rev. and Mrs. Bruce F. Hunt have announced the engagement of their daughter, Lois Margaret, to Mr. John J. Mitchell of Cary, N. C. Mr. Mitchell is a student at Westminster Seminary. The wedding is to take place in December.

Santa Cruz Church Formed

At the meeting of the Presbytery of California held in Sunnyvale, Calif. on May 12 and previously reported in the GUARDIAN, the Rev. Rousas J. Rushdoony, pictured below, was received and a new Orthodox Presbyterian Church organized, consisting of a number of persons who had separated from the Presbyterian Church in the U.S.A. in Santa Cruz.

The new Church was organized in response to the following petition, signed by 66 individuals:

"We the undersigned, as charter members, do hereby petition to be organized as an Orthodox Presbyterian Church in Santa Cruz, California, and the Rev. R. J. Rushdoony ordained and called as our pastor.

"We affirm our faith in Scripture as the only infallible and inspired Word of God, the rule and guide of faith. We declare our belief in the sovereignty of God, and we find therein our security and refuge. We believe that man can only be saved by faith

The Rev. R. J. Rushdoony

THE DOMINIONISTS

THE SECOND HALF OF THE TWENTIETH century was a time of steady decline for conservative Protestant denominations in the United States. Despite the efforts of evangelists and political action groups such as the Moral Majority, the percentage of Americans who belonged to a Protestant church declined from over 75 percent at mid-century to less than 50 percent as the century ended, and conservatives suffered defeat after defeat on issues such as divorce, abortion, and same-sex marriage. In response, some evangelical Protestants set out to overthrow American democracy and replace it with a religious dictatorship.

Dominionism, as this movement is called, drew its inspiration from the writings of Rev. Rousas J. Rushdoony (1916–2001), whose *Institutes of Biblical Law* (1973) called for the abolition of civil rights, the return of slavery, and the mass murder of religious dissidents.

The most influential Dominionist movement, the Coalition on Revival (COR), was founded in 1984; its founders pledged to give their lives to impose a totalitarian Christian theocracy on America. While its members denounce secret societies such as Masonry, the COR, which still exists, functions as a secret society itself, training ministers and other leaders in the arts of political subversion, and producing propaganda that pushes the abolition of the Bill of Rights and other constitutional freedoms.

So far, at least, the Dominionists have remained a small splinter group, and their efforts have yet to convince any significant number of American Christians to turn their back on the Constitution. Its existence shows, however, that the long history of conservative American conspiracies is not over yet.

SEE ALSO: The Know-Nothing Party (1849), The Klan Reborn (1915)

A photo of the Reverend Rousas J. Rushdoony accompanying an article published by *The Presbyterian Guardian* newsletter in July 1958, announcing Rushdoony's formation of "a new Orthodox Presbyterian Church . . . consisting of a number of persons who had separated from the Presbyterian Church in the U.S.A." As the father of "Christian Reconstructionism," Rushdoony is credited with inspiring the Christian homeschooling movement, among other accomplishments.

THE NEW WORLD ORDER

To President George H. W. Bush (b. 1924), it was probably just a convenient turn of phrase. On January 16, 1991, as American aircraft carried out the first bombing raids against Baghdad in the opening hours of Operation Desert Storm, Bush gave a speech proclaiming a "new world order" in which an alliance of industrial nations would unite to counter military aggression on the part of Third World nations around the world. In all probability, he and his speechwriters were startled when that phrase suddenly got taken up by conspiracy researchers around the globe.

The phrase "new world order" already had a significant presence in conspiracy literature before Bush used it. John Birch Society founder Robert Welch Jr. (1899–1985) coined it in 1972 to describe the global police state that he believed elite circles of "insiders" planned to impose on the world. From John Birch Society literature, the phrase found its way into various corners of the far right, and then leapt to the far left after the publication of *Trilateralism* by Holly Sklar (b. 1955) in 1980.

Bush's use of the phrase thus convinced the conspiracy-minded across the political spectrum that the dystopian future they feared had already been proclaimed, and gave an additional boost to already widespread fears. Further fuel for the blaze was added by the Bush administration's pet philosopher Francis Fukuyama (b. 1952), whose 1989 manifesto *The End of History and the Last Man* proclaimed the supposedly permanent triumph of corporate capitalism and country-club Republican politics. The rhetoric of the new world order has thus become an important keynote in conspiracy literature in recent decades, and will doubtless maintain that status for decades to come.

SEE ALSO: The John Birch Society (1959), *Trilateralism* (1980)

President George H. W. Bush and First Lady Barbara Bush (1925-2018) wave from the back of a vehicle during a Thanksgiving Day visit, in 1990, to U.S. troops stationed in Saudi Arabia for Operation Desert Shield. A couple of months later, on January 16, 1991, when President Bush announced the start of Operation Desert Storm, he used the expression "new world order" in his speech. That phrase still resonated at the time with conspiracy theorists and elicited a good deal of interest from them, much to the dismay of the president's speechwriters.

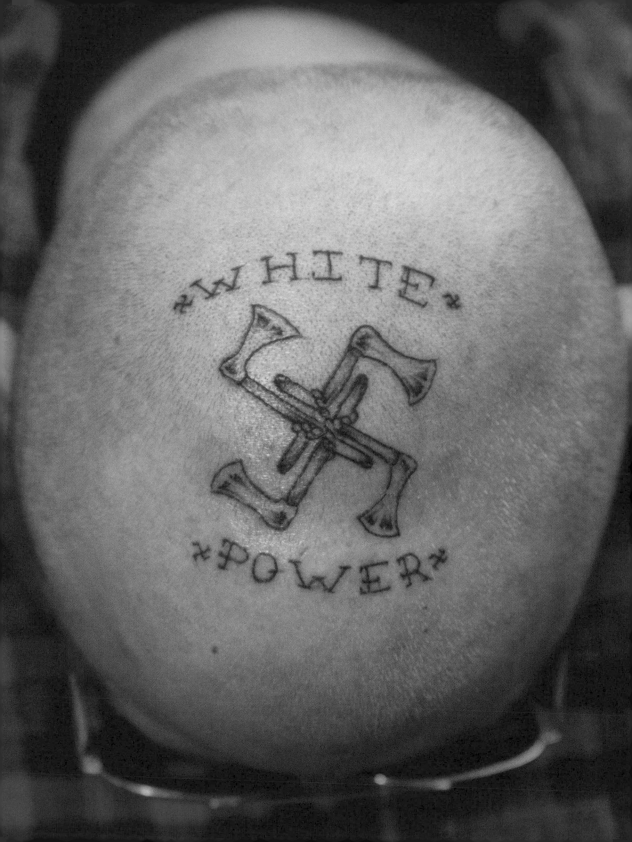

THE WHITE ORDER OF THULE

1994

BY THE LAST DECADE OF THE TWENTIETH century, the neo-Nazi movement had established itself across the industrial world, but remained divided among many competing organizations. That concerned Kerry Bolton, a New Zealander who headed the fascist Nationalist Workers Party in the 1980s. In 1994, together with a network of neo-Nazis in Europe, Australia, New Zealand, and the United States, he founded a secret society—originally called the Black Order— to spread the neo-Nazi gospel in popular culture across the Western world using the industrial-music scene, political parties on the far right, and the fascist end of occultism as routes of influence.

In 1997, the absurdity of a white supremacist organization calling itself the Black Order finally sank in, and the order renamed itself the White Order of Thule—a reference to the Thule Society, the secret society that founded the Nazi Party in the 1920s, and also to the body of neo-Nazi mythology surrounding the supposed lost continent of Thule. In the same year, it moved its headquarters from Wellington, New Zealand, to Richmond, Virginia; in 2001, it moved again to a suburb of Spokane, Washington.

So far, the major activities of the White Order of Thule have consisted of a quarterly magazine, a publishing program that keeps racist and fascist literature in print, and networking opportunities for its members. The spread of neo-Nazi ideas through the crawl spaces of popular culture, however, suggests that its efforts may be having a significant effect.

SEE ALSO: The Thule Society (1918), Neo-Nazi Secret Societies (1945), The American Renaissance Party (1949)

The influence of neo-Nazi and white supremacist organizations like the White Order of Thule can be seen all too clearly in this photo of a man with a "white power" tattoo. He displayed the design at the USA Nationalist Party rally, a gathering of skinheads, neo-Nazis, and Ku Klux Klan members in Washington Crossing, Pennsylvania, on November 6, 1993.

Further Reading

c. 975 BCE: The Temple of Solomon
Hamblin, William James, and David Rolph Seely, *Solomon's Temple: Myth and History* (London: Thames & Hudson, 2007).
Lundquist, John M., *The Temple of Jerusalem: Past, Present, and Future* (Westport, CT: Praeger, 2008).

6th century BCE: The Pythagorean Brotherhood
Ferguson, Kitty, *The Pythagorean Brotherhood* (New York: Walker, 2011).

1st century CE: The Gnostics
Barnstone, Willis, and Marvin Meyer, *The Gnostic Bible* (Boston: Shambhala, 2003).
Filoramo, Giovanni, *A History of Gnosticism* (Oxford: Blackwell, 1990).

1030: The Cathars
Lambert, Malcolm, *Medieval Heresy* (Oxford: Blackwell, 1992).
O'Shea, Stephen, *The Perfect Heresy: The Life and Death of the Cathars* (London: Profile, 2011).

1307: Fall of the Knights Templar
Barber, Malcolm, *The Trial of the Templars* (Cambridge: Cambridge University Press, 1978).
Partner, Peter, *The Murdered Magicians: The Knights Templar and their Myth* (Oxford: Oxford University Press, 1991).

c. 1390: The Regius Manuscript
Knoop, D., and G.P. Jones, *The Genesis of Freemasonry* (Manchester: Manchester University Press, 1947).

c. 1400: The Adamites
Lambert, Malcolm, *Medieval Heresy* (Oxford: Blackwell, 1992).

1511: The Alumbrados
Hamilton, Alastair, *Heresy and Mysticism in Sixteenth-Century Spain: The Alumbrados* (Cambridge: James Clarke, 1992).

1555: The Family of Love
Hamilton, Alastair, *The Family of Love* (Cambridge: James Clarke, 1981).

1598: The Schaw Statutes
Stevenson, David, *The Origins of Freemasonry: Scotland's Century* (Cambridge: Cambridge University Press, 1988).

1614: The Rosicrucians
McIntosh, Christopher, *The Rosicrucians* (York Beach, ME: Samuel Weiser, 1997).
Yates, Frances, *The Rosicrucian Enlightenment* (London: Routledge & Kegan Paul, 1972).

1646: Elias Ashmole Becomes a Mason
Churton, Tobias, Magus: *The Invisible Life of Elias Ashmole* (Lichfield: Signal, 2004).

1688: The Glorious Revolution
McLynn, Frank J., *The Jacobites* (London: Routledge and Kegan Paul, 1985).
Szechi, Daniel, *The Jacobites: Britain and Europe 1688–1788* (Manchester: Manchester University Press, 1994).

c. 1710: The Chevaliers of Jubilation
Jacob, Margaret, *The Radical Enlightenment* (London: George Allen and Unwin, 1981).

1715: The 'Fifteen
McLynn, Frank J., *The Jacobites* (London: Routledge and Kegan Paul, 1985).
Szechi, Daniel, *The Jacobites: Britain and Europe 1688–1788* (Manchester: Manchester University Press, 1994).

1717: The First Masonic Grand Lodge
Knoop, D., and G. P. Jones, *The Genesis of Freemasonry* (Manchester: Manchester University Press, 1947).
Ridley, Jasper, *The Freemasons* (New York: Arcade, 2011).

1724: The Gormogons
Uglow, Jenny, *William Hogarth: A Life and a World* (London: Faber and Faber, 2011).

1736: Ramsay's Oration
Partner, Peter, *The Murdered Magicians: The Knights Templar and their Myth* (Oxford: Oxford University Press, 1991).

Szechi, Daniel, *The Jacobites: Britain and Europe 1688–1788* (Manchester: Manchester University Press, 1994).

1738: *In Eminente*
Jacob, Margaret C., *Living the Enlightenment: Freemasonry and Politics in Eighteenth-Century Europe* (Oxford: Oxford University Press, 1991)
Ridley, Jasper, *The Freemasons* (New York: Arcade, 2011).

1745: The 'Forty-Five
McLynn, Frank J., *The Jacobites* (London: Routledge and Kegan Paul, 1985).

Szechi, Daniel, *The Jacobites: Britain and Europe 1688–1788* (Manchester: Manchester University Press, 1994).

1746: The Hell-Fire Club
Towers, Eric, *Dashwood: The Man and the Myth* (Wellingborough, UK: Aquarian, 1986).

1751: The Ancient-Modern Schism
Jacob, Margaret C., *Living the Enlightenment: Freemasonry and Politics in Eighteenth-Century Europe* (Oxford University Press, 1991).
Ridley, Jasper, *The Freemasons* (New York: Arcade, 2011).

1754: The Strict Observance
de Hoyos, Arturo, and Alan Bernheim, "Introduction to the Rituals of the Strict Observance," *Heredom* 14 (2006), 47–104.
Harrison, David, *The Lost Rites and Rituals of Freemasonry* (Addlestone, UK: Lewis Masonic, 2017).

1755: The Golden and Rosy Cross
Susanna Åkerman, *Rose Cross Over the Baltic: The Spread of Rosicrucianism in Northern Europe* (Brill: Leiden, 1998).
McIntosh, Christopher, *The Rose Cross and the Age of Reason* (New York: E.J. Brill, 1992).

1760: The Committees of Correspondence
Maier, Pauline R., *From Resistance to Revolution: Colonial Radicals and the Development of American Opposition to Britain, 1765–1776* (New York: Knopf, 1972).
Standiford, Les, *Desperate Sons: Samuel Adams, Patrick Henry, John Hancock, and the Secret Bands of Radicals Who Led the Colonies to War* (New York: HarperCollins, 2012).

1765: The Sons of Liberty
Carp, Benjamin L., *Defiance of the Patriots: The Boston Tea Party and the Making of America* (New Haven: Yale University Press, 2010).
Unger, Harlow Giles, *American Tempest: How the Boston Tea Party Sparked a Revolution* (Cambridge, MA: Da Capo, 2011).

1770: The Illuminés of Avignon
Roberts, J. M., *The Mythology of the Secret Societies* (New York: Scribner, 1972).

1776: The Bavarian Illuminati
Melanson, Terry, *Perfectibilists: the 18th Century Bavarian Order of the Illuminati* (Chicago: Trine Day, 2009).
Roberts, J. M., *The Mythology of the Secret Societies* (New York: Scribner, 1972).

1782: The Convention of Wilhelmsbad
Jacob, Margaret C., *Living the Enlightenment: Freemasonry and Politics in Eighteenth-Century Europe* (Oxford University Press, 1991).

1789: The French Revolution
Lefebvre, Georges, *The Coming of the French Revolution* (Princeton, NJ: Princeton University Press, 1947).
Schama, Simon, *Citizens: A Chronicle of the French Revolution* (New York: Knopf, 1989).

1790: The Social Circle
Billington, James H., *Fire in the Minds of Men: Origins of the Revolutionary Faith* (New York: Basic, 1980).

1796: The Conspiracy of Equals
Billington, James H., *Fire in the Minds of Men: Origins of the Revolutionary Faith* (New York: Basic, 1980).

1797: The Philadelphes
Billington, James H., *Fire in the Minds of Men: Origins of the Revolutionary Faith* (New York: Basic, 1980).

1797: The Raggi
Billington, James H., *Fire in the Minds of Men: Origins of the Revolutionary Faith* (New York: Basic, 1980).

1797: *Proofs of a Conspiracy*
Roberts, J. M., *The Mythology of the Secret Societies* (New York: Scribner, 1972).
Robison, John, *Proofs of a Conspiracy against all the Religions and Governments of Europe: carried on in the Secret Meetings of Free Masons, Illuminati, and Reading Societies* (Bloomington, IL: Masonic Book Club, 2009).

1800: The Carbonari
Billington, James H., *Fire in the Minds of Men: Origins of the Revolutionary Faith* (New York: Basic, 1980).
Stites, Richard, *The Four Horsemen: Riding to Liberty in Post-Napoleonic Europe* (New York: Oxford University Press, 2014).

1809: The Sublime Perfect Masters
Billington, James H., *Fire in the Minds of Men: Origins of the Revolutionary Faith* (New York: Basic, 1980).

1825: The Decembrists
Raeff, Marc, *The Decembrist Movement* (Englewood Cliffs, NJ: Prentice-Hall, 1966).
Stites, Richard, *The Four Horsemen: Riding to Liberty in Post-Napoleonic Europe* (New York: Oxford University Press, 2014).

1826: The Morgan Affair
Palmer, John C., *The Morgan Affair and Anti-Masonry* (Kingsport, TN: Southern, 1946).
Vaughn, William Preston, *The Anti-Masonic Party in the United States: 1826–1843* (Lexington: University of Kentucky Press, 1983).

1828: The Anti-Masonic Party
Vaughn, William Preston, *The Anti-Masonic Party in the United States:1826–1843* (Lexington: University of Kentucky Press, 1983).

1832: Skull and Bones
Robbins, Alexandra, *Secrets of the Tomb: Skull and Bones, the Ivy League, and the Secret Paths of Power* (Boston: Little, Brown, 2002).

1834: The League of Outlaws
Billington, James H., *Fire in the Minds of Men: Origins of the Revolutionary Faith* (New York: Basic, 1980).

1837: The League of the Just
Billington, James H., *Fire in the Minds of Men: Origins of the Revolutionary Faith* (New York: Basic, 1980).

1847: *The Communist Manifesto*
Engels, Friedrich, and Karl Marx, *The Communist Manifesto* (London: Penguin, 2015).
Pipes, Richard, *Communism: A History* (New York: Modern Library, 2003).

1849: The Know-Nothing Party
Bennett, David H., *The Party of Fear: From Nativist Movements to the New Right in American History* (Chapel Hill: University of North Carolina Press, 1988).
Billington, Ray Allen, *The Protestant Crusade 1800–1860* (Chicago: Quadrangle, 1952).

1854: The Knights of the Golden Circle
Benton, Elbert J., *The Movement for Peace Without a Victory in the Civil War* (New York: Da Capo, 1972).
Gray, Wood, *The Hidden Civil War: The Story of the Copperheads* (New York: Viking, 1942).

1855: The Nihilists
Broido, Vera, *Apostles Into Terrorists* (New York: Viking, 1977).
Hingley, Ronald, *Nihilists: Russian Radicals and Revolutionaries in the Reign of Alexander II* (New York: Delacorte, 1967).

1858: The Fenian Brotherhood
O Concubhair, Padraig, *"The Fenians Were Dreadful Men": The 1867 Rising* (Cork: Mercier, 2011).

1863: The Order of American Knights
Benton, Elbert J., *The Movement for Peace Without a Victory in the Civil War* (New York: Da Capo, 1972).
Gray, Wood, *The Hidden Civil War: The Story of the Copperheads* (New York: Viking, 1942).

1864: The First International
Billington, James H., *Fire in the Minds of Men: Origins of the Revolutionary Faith* (New York: Basic, 1980).
Drachkovitch, Milorad M., *The Revolutionary Internationals, 1864–1943* (Stanford: Stanford University Press, 1966).

1865: The Ku Klux Klan
Newton, Michael, *White Robes and Burning Crosses: A History of the Ku Klux Klan from 1866* (Jefferson, NC: McFarland, 2014).
Wade, Wyn Craig, *The Fiery Cross: The Ku Klux Klan in America* (New York: Simon & Schuster, 1987).

1866: The International Brothers
Billington, James H., *Fire in the Minds of Men: Origins of the Revolutionary Faith* (New York: Basic, 1980).

1869: The Knights of Labor
Phelan, Craig, *Grand Master Workman: Terence Powderly and the Knights of Labor* (Westport, CT: Greenwood, 2000).

1871: The Shriners
van Deventer, Fred, *Parade to Glory* (New York: Pyramid, 1964).

1878: The Bohemian Grove
Domhoff, G. William, *The Bohemian Grove and Other Retreats* (New York: Harper & Row, 1974).

c. 1880: The Mafia Comes to America
Fox, Stephen, *Blood and Power: Organized Crime in Twentieth-Century America* (New York: Morrow, 1989).

1886: The Order of the White Rose
McLynn, Frank J., *The Jacobites* (London: Routledge and Kegan Paul, 1985).

1887: The Fabian Society
Mackenzie, Norman, and Jeanne Mackenzie, *The Fabians* (New York: Simon and Schuster, 1977).

1887: The American Protective Association
Bennett, David H., *The Party of Fear: From Nativist Movements to the New Right in American History* (Chapel Hill: University of North Carolina Press, 1988).
Kinzer, Donald L., *An Episode in Anti-Catholicism: The American Protective Association* (Seattle: University of Washington Press, 1964).

1889: The Second International
Drachkovitch, Milorad M., *The Revolutionary Internationals, 1864–1943* (Stanford: Stanford University Press, 1966).

1895: *The Protocols of the Elders of Zion*
Cohn, Norman, *Warrant for Genocide* (New York: Harper & Row, 1967).

1897: The "Palladian Order" Hoax
Waite, Arthur Edward, *Devil Worship in France* (York Beach, ME: Weiser, 2003).

1905: The Black Hundreds
Cohn, Norman, *Warrant for Genocide* (New York: Harper & Row, 1967).
Laqueur, Walter, *Black Hundred: The Rise of the Extreme Right in Russia* (New York: HarperPerennial, 1994).

1907: The Order of New Templars
Angebert, Jean-Michel, *The Occult and the Third Reich: The Mystical Origins of Nazism and the Search for the Holy Grail* (New York: Macmillan, 1974).
Goodrick-Clarke, Nicholas, *The Occult Roots of Nazism: Secret Aryan Cults and Their Influence on Nazi Ideology* (New York: New York University Press, 1992).

1908: Ariosophy
Angebert, Jean-Michel, *The Occult and the Third Reich: The Mystical Origins of Nazism and the Search for the Holy Grail* (New York: Macmillan, 1974).
Goodrick-Clarke, Nicholas, *The Occult Roots of Nazism: Secret Aryan Cults and Their Influence on Nazi Ideology* (New York: New York University Press, 1992).

1912: The Germanenorden
Angebert, Jean-Michel, *The Occult and the Third Reich: The Mystical Origins of Nazism and the Search for the Holy Grail* (New York: Macmillan, 1974).
Goodrick-Clarke, Nicholas, *The Occult Roots of Nazism: Secret Aryan Cults and Their Influence on Nazi Ideology* (New York: New York University Press, 1992).

1915: The Klan Reborn
Newton, Michael, *White Robes and Burning Crosses: A History of the Ku Klux Klan from 1866* (Jefferson, NC: McFarland, 2014).
Wade, Wyn Craig, *The Fiery Cross: The Ku Klux Klan in America* (New York: Simon & Schuster, 1987).

1916: The Easter Rising
Foy, Michael, and Brian Barton, *The Easter Rising* (Stroud, UK: Tempus, 2011).
Thompson, William Irwin, *Easter 1916: The Imagination of an Insurrection* (New York: Barnes & Noble, 2009).

1917: The American Protective League
Mills, Bill, *The League* (New York: Skyhorse, 2011).

1917: The Russian Revolution
Moorehead, Alan, *The Russian Revolution* (New York: Carroll and Graf, 1990).
Smith, S.A., *The Russian Revolution* (New York: Sterling, 2011).

1918: The Thule Society
Angebert, Jean-Michel, *The Occult and the Third Reich: The Mystical Origins of Nazism and the Search for the Holy Grail* (New York: Macmillan, 1974).
Goodrick-Clarke, Nicholas, *The Occult Roots of Nazism: Secret Aryan Cults and Their Influence on Nazi Ideology* (New York: New York University Press, 1992).

1919: The Third International
Drachkovitch, Milorad M., *The Revolutionary Internationals, 1864–1943* (Stanford: Stanford University Press, 1966).

1920: Prohibition
Behr, Edward, *Prohibition: Thirteen Years That Changed America* (New York: Arcade, 1996).
Fox, Stephen, *Blood and Power: Organized Crime in Twentieth-Century America* (New York: Morrow, 1989).

1921: The Council on Foreign Relations
Goldberg, Robert Alan, *Enemies Within: The Culture of Conspiracy in Modern America* (New Haven: Yale University Press, 2001).
Schulzinger, Robert D., *The Wise Men of Foreign Affairs* (New York: Columbia University Press, 1984).

1925: The SS
Höhne, Heinrich, *The Order of the Death's Head* (London: Pan, 1972).
Lumsden, Robin, *Himmler's Black Order* (Stroud, UK: Sutton, 1997).

1925: The Klan Destroyed
Newton, Michael, *White Robes and Burning Crosses: A History of the Ku Klux Klan from 1866* (Jefferson, NC: McFarland, 2014).
Wade, Wyn Craig, *The Fiery Cross: The Ku Klux Klan in America* (New York: Simon & Schuster, 1987).

1928: Opus Dei
Allen, John L., *Opus Dei* (New York: Doubleday, 2005).

1929: Al Capone becomes *Capo dei Capi*
Fox, Stephen, *Blood and Power: Organized Crime in Twentieth-Century America* (New York: Morrow, 1989).
Kobler, John, *Capone: The Life and Times of Al Capone* (New York: Da Capo, 2003).

1933: Hitler Takes Power
Evans, Richard J., *The Coming of the Third Reich* (London: Allen Lane, 2003).
Kershaw, Ian, *Hitler, 1889–1936: Hubris* (New York: Norton, 1998).

1945: Neo-Nazi Secret Societies
Goodrick-Clarke, Nicholas, *Black Sun: Aryan Cults, Esoteric Nazism, and the Politics of Identity* (New York: New York University Press, 2002).

1946: *Propaganda Due* (P2)
DiFonzo, Luigi, *St. Peter's Banker* (New York: Franklin Watts, 1983).
Willan, Philip, *The Last Supper: The Mafia, the Masons and the Killing of Roberto Calvi* (London: Constable & Robinson, 2007).

1948: The Mau Maus
Edgerton, Robert B., *Mau Mau: An African Crucible* (New York: Free Press, 1989).
Majdalany, Fred, *State of Emergency: The Full Story of Mau Mau* (Boston: Houghton Mifflin, 1963).

1949: The National Renaissance Party
Goodrick-Clarke, Nicholas, *Black Sun: Aryan Cults, Esoteric Nazism, and the Politics of Identity* (New York: New York University Press, 2002).

1954: The Bilderbergers
Goldberg, Robert Alan, *Enemies Within: The Culture of Conspiracy in Modern America* (New Haven: Yale University Press, 2001).

1956: The Priory of Sion
Baigent, Michael, Richard Leigh, and Henry
Lincoln, *Holy Blood, Holy Grail* (New York:
Dell, 1983).
Richardson, Robert, *The Unknown Treasure*
(Houston: NorthStar, 1998).

1959: The John Birch Society
Goldberg, Robert Alan, *Enemies Within: The
Culture of Conspiracy in Modern America*
(New Haven: Yale University Press, 2001).
Grove, Gene, *Inside the John Birch Society*
(Greenwich, CT: Fawcett, 1961).

1968: The Club of Rome
Meadows, Donnella, David Meadows, Jorgen
Randers, and William W. Behrens III, *The
Limits to Growth* (New York: Universe, 1972).

1980: Trilateralism
Goldberg, Robert Alan, *Enemies Within: The
Culture of Conspiracy in Modern America*
(New Haven: Yale University Press, 2001).
Sklar, Holly, *Trilateralism: The Trilateral
Commission and Elite Planning for World
Management* (Boston: South End Press,
1980).

1983: The Order
Flynn, Kevin, and Gary Gerhardt, *The Silent
Brotherhood: Inside America's Racist
Underground* (New York: Free Press,
1989).

1984: The Dominionists
Barron, Bruce, *Heaven on Earth?* (Grand
Rapids, MI: Zondervan, 1992).

1991: The New World Order
Goldberg, Robert Alan, *Enemies Within: The
Culture of Conspiracy in Modern America*
(New Haven: Yale University Press, 2001).

1994: The White Order of Thule
Goodrick-Clarke, Nicholas, *Black Sun: Aryan
Cults, Esoteric Nazism, and the Politics of
Identity* (New York: New York University
Press, 2002).

INDEX

IMAGE CREDITS

ABOUT THE AUTHOR

John Michael Greer is one of the most widely respected writers and scholars in the occult field today. The author of more than forty books, including *The New Encyclopedia of the Occult*, he served for twelve years as Grand Archdruid of the Ancient Order of Druids in America (AODA). He lives in Cumberland, Maryland, with his wife, Sara.